John Gill

Classics of Reformed Spirituality

"Bespangled with divine grace":
The spirituality of John Gill

Michael A.G. Haykin, series editor

Classics of Reformed Spirituality

"Bespangled with divine grace"

The spirituality of John Gill

Edited by

Michael A.G. Haykin & Phil Cotnoir

with Allen R. Mickle and Roger D. Duke

press

Bespangled with divine grace
Copyright © Michael A.G. Haykin and Phil Cotnoir 2022

Published by: Joshua Press, West Lorne, Ontario
www.JoshuaPress.com

Cover illustration by Deborah Livingston-Lowe
Front cover portrait of John Gill by Ellie Best-Shaw

All rights reserved. This book or any portion thereof may not be reproduced or used in any manner whatsoever without the express written permission of the publisher except for the use of brief quotations in a book review.

Paperback ISBN: 978-1-77484-078-8
Ebook ISBN: 978-1-77484-079-5

Dedication

To Rick & Carolyn Egelton
and to Stephen & Karen Swallow,
for their Christian friendship
and support over the years.

—Michael

To my father David
and the memory of my mother Ginette.
From Dad I learned the love of reading books;
from Mom the love of words and writing.
These two loves set me firmly on the path
I am on today.

—Phil

No "rose of Sharon" can be more beautiful in color and delightful to the eye than the church is in the eyes of Christ, as she is clothed with his pure and spotless righteousness, adorned with the graces of his Spirit, and standing at his right-hand in cloth of gold, bespangled with the sparkling gems of divine grace. Her beauty is desirable to him, she being in his eye "the fairest among women."

John Gill, commentary on Song of Songs 2:1

Contents

17
"The great & good Dr Gill":
an introduction to his life and spirituality

31
Chronology

37
The satisfaction of Christ

39
The resurrection of the body

43
Applying unto God for mercy

47
The blessedness of those who have
imputed righteousness

51
The Gospel

55
Sanctification

57
Of communion with God

63
Of the public ministry of the Word

65
Christ on the cross

69
The Church as the "rose of Sharon"

73
The Church as the lily of the valley

77
Christ in the lily of the valley

81
The first and chief commandment

83
Bless the Lord, O my soul

87
Blessed are the merciful

91
Seeing the beauty of God

93
How angels serve believers

95
The Trinity transforms our worship, prayer, and unity

99
Distinctions in the Trinity

103
The Trinity is essential

107
Grace and truth in Christ

111
Longing to know Christ more

115
The presence of God

119
How God's presence is lost and how it is found

121
The end of all things

125
What is prayer?

127
Some instructions on prayer

131
Further directions on prayer

133
Encouragements to prayer

137
Christ the Saviour from the tempest

141
On faith, hope, and love

145
Christ is life

147
A principle of grace in the heart

151
Dying thoughts

155
Last words

157
Appendix 1

171
Appendix 2

185
Reading Spiritual Classics

189
Select Bibliography

193
Scripture Index

"The great & good Dr Gill": an introduction to his life and spirituality

Michael A.G. Haykin

John Gill (1697–1771) was born in Kettering, Northamptonshire, in 1697, at the very close of the Puritan era. In the earliest memoir of his life, probably written by his son-in-law, George Keith, mention is made of a prophecy that occurred at the time of Gill's birth. Apparently, on the day that Gill was born, a forester by the name of Chambers came to his parent's home to deliver some wood. As Edward Gill was joyously telling the forester that he had had a son born that very morning, a passing stranger was overheard to say, according to the forester, "Yes, and he will be a scholar too, and all the world cannot hinder it."[1] If this did happen, and the author of

---

[1] [George Keith,] "A Summary of the Life, Writings, and Character, Of the late Reverend and learned John Gill, D.D." in John Gill, *A Collection of Sermons and Tracts* (London: George Keith, 1773), 1:x. For other studies of Gill's life and

this memoir definitely believed that it did, it would have been a comfort to Gill's parents when their son's early schooling at a local grammar school came to an abrupt end in 1708, for the school's headmaster demanded that all of his pupils attend Anglican morning prayer. Gill's parents were adamant Dissenters and consequently withdrew their son from the school.[2] As the family was unable to afford to send their young son to a Dissenting Academy—Gill's father Edward was a wool merchant—Gill's formal education was over. But this did not at all

---

thought, see John Rippon, *A Brief Memoir of the Life and Writings of the late Rev. John Gill, D.D.* (1838, Harrisonburg, VA: Gano Books, 1992); Graham Harrison, *Dr. John Gill and His Teaching*, Annual Lecture of The Evangelical Library (London: The Evangelical Library, 1971); George M. Ella, *John Gill and the Cause of God and Truth* (Eggleston, Co. Durham: Go Publications, 1995); Robert W. Oliver, "John Gill: Orthodox Dissenter," *The Strict Baptist Historical Society Bulletin* 23 (1996): 3–18; Michael A.G. Haykin, ed., *The Life and Thought of John Gill (1697–1771): A Tercentennial Appreciation* (Leiden: E.J. Brill, 1997); and Timothy George, "John Gill" in *Theologians of the Baptist Tradition*, ed. Timothy George and David S. Dockery, Rev. ed. (Nashville, TN: Broadman & Holman, 2001), 11–33. See also the collection of articles on Gill in *The Southern Baptist Journal of Theology* 25, no.1 (Spring 2021).

[2] The Dissenters were those Christians who disagreed with the Church of England on various matters and formed their own churches and other institutions.

quench that insatiable hunger for learning which proved to be one of his enduring qualities. In fact, "such a thing is as sure as John Gill is in the bookseller's shop" became a saying in Kettering during his teen years.[3]

Gill had acquired a good foundation in Latin and Greek before leaving the grammar school. And by the age of nineteen, he was not only adept in both of these languages but also well on the way to becoming proficient in Hebrew. Knowledge of these three languages gave him ready access to a wealth of Scriptural and theological knowledge, which he used to great advantage in the years that followed as he pastored Goat Yard Chapel, Southwark (later Carter Lane Baptist Church), in the city of London from 1719 until his death in 1771.

"As surely as Dr Gill is in his study"[4]

During his 52-year-long pastorate, Gill wrote a number of significant works. The first was an exposition of the Song of Songs (1728), which

---

[3] [Keith,] "Summary" in Gill, *Sermons and Tracts*, 1:x.
[4] A common saying apparently during Gill's London pastorate. See [Keith,] "Summary" in Gill, *Sermons and Tracts*, 1:x, note a.

Gill approached from a traditional interpretative vantage point, namely, that it was to be read as a love song between Christ and his church, which, according to John Rippon (1751–1836), who succeeded him as pastor, "served very much to make Mr. Gill known."[5] Then, in the late 1730s, Gill issued a robust defence of the so-called five points of Calvinism, *The Cause of God and Truth* (1735–1738). Written at a time when English Calvinism was very much a house in disarray, it secured for Gill a reputation as a prominent defender of the Reformed cause and revealed his deep indebtedness to seventeenth-century Reformed thought.[6] The story is told that when Gill was about to send this defence of Calvinism to the press, one of the members of his church told him in no uncertain terms that the publication of the book would lead to the loss of some of Gill's best friends as well as the loss of income. Gill's reply was terse and gracious, but very much to the point: "I can afford

---

[5] Rippon, *Brief Memoir*, 24. For selections from this work, see below, selections 10, 11, and 12.

[6] For details of this indebtedness, see Richard Muller, "John Gill and the Reformed Tradition" in *Life and Thought of John Gill*, ed. Haykin, 51–68.

to be poor," he said, "but I cannot afford to injure my conscience."[7]

This memorable anecdote says much about the man and captures a central reason for his greatness as a Christian theologian. He had a tenacious determination to stay the course when it came to cleaving to biblical truth, refusing to be shaped by pragmatic concerns. What mattered above all was the truth and its proclamation. Later in his life, when Gill published a robust critique of the views of John Wesley (1703–1791) on the perseverance of the saints and predestination, Wesley referred to Gill as one who "fights for his opinions through thick and thin."[8]

The 1740s saw the publication of Gill's critical commentary on the entire New Testament—his profoundly learned *Exposition of the New Testament*, published in three folio volumes between 1746 and 1748. Gill's companion to this commentary, his four-volume *Exposition of the Old Testament* did not appear for another fifteen

---

[7] Quoted C.H. Spurgeon, *Autobiography*, ed. Susannah Spurgeon and Joseph Harrald, Rev. ed. (Edinburgh; Carlisle, PA: Banner of Truth, 1973), 2:477.

[8] Cited George, "John Gill," 18.

years or so (1763–1766).⁹ Together, these two sets became a central feature of the libraries of Baptist ministers throughout the British Isles. Also occupying a prominent place in those libraries was Gill's *magnum opus*, *A Body of Doctrinal and Practical Divinity*, issued in 1769–1770, which was the definitive codification of his theological perspective.¹⁰

It is noteworthy that when William Williams Pantycelyn (1717–1791), one of the central figures of eighteenth-century Welsh Calvinistic Methodism and the author of "Guide me, O thou great Jehovah," was dying in 1791, he thanked God for the "true religion" that he had found particularly in the writings of "Dr. Goodwin, Dr. Owen, Dr. Gill, Marshall, Harvey, [and] Usher."¹¹ Four of these authors are Puritans: the two leading Independent theologians, Thomas Goodwin (1600–1679) and John Owen (1616–

---

⁹ For selections from his three-volume commentary on the New Testament, see below, selections 15, 16, 21, 22, 25, 31, and 32. For selections from his four-volume commentary on the Old Testament, see below, selections 3, 9, 13, and 14.

¹⁰ For selections from his *A Body of Doctrinal and Practical Divinity*, see below, selections 1, 2, 5, 6, 7, 8, 17, 18, 19, 20, 26, and 29.

¹¹ Cited Eifion Evans, "William Williams of Pant Y Celyn," *The Evangelical Library Bulletin* 42 (Spring, 1969): 6.

83), the Anglo-Irish Episcopalian James Ussher (1581–1656), and the English Presbyterian Walter Marshall (1628–1680). "Harvey" is the Anglican Calvinist James Hervey (1714–1758), one of the members of the Wesleys' Holy Club, famous in his day for a defence of Calvinism, *Theron and Aspasio* (1755), and a close friend of Gill. That Gill should appear in the company of four Puritans says much about his way of doing theology as well as the form of his publications. In a day when brevity was highly prized as a literary quality, Gill's works read and looked like the massive tomes of the baroque print culture of the Puritan era. This may have had something to do with Gill's character. As Rippon noted in his memoir of Gill, "The Doctor considered not any subject superficially, or by halves. As deeply as human sagacity, enlightened by grace, could penetrate, he went to the bottom of everything he engaged in."[12] It also reflected Gill's deep love for the Word of God and his characteristically Puritan conviction that the whole of divine revelation needed to be taught to the people of God.

But for some of his contemporaries, Gill's penchant for systematic theology was off-

---

[12] Rippon, *Brief Memoir*, 137.

putting. Surely it is a lack of interest in the systematizing of Christian thought that lies behind the famous remark of the younger Robert Hall (1764–1831) about Gill's writings. Hall was once in conversation with the Welsh Baptist preacher Christmas Evans (1766–1838) when the latter expressed his admiration for Gill and said that he wished that Gill's works had been written in Welsh. Hall, ever the vivacious conversationalist, quickly retorted, "I wish they had, sir; I wish they had with all my heart, for then I should never have read them. They are a continent of mud, sir."[13] In point of fact, this singularly unfair remark tells us more about Hall than it does about Gill. Very few of those who read Gill in the eighteenth century would have described his work thus, even those who were critical of some of Gill's theological emphases, like Andrew Fuller (1754–1815). For many, he was "the great & good Dr Gill," as the hymnwriter Augustus

---

[13] Cited Olinthus Gregory, "A Brief Memoir of the Rev. Robert Hall, A.M." in *The Works of the Rev. Robert Hall, A.M.*, ed. Olinthus Gregory (New York, NY: Harper & Brothers, 1854), 82. By contrast, John Collett Ryland felt that the study of Gill's theology led one into "an ocean of divinity" (cited W.R. Estep, Jr., "Gill, John" in *Encyclopedia of Southern Baptists* (Nashville, TN: Broadman Press, 1958), 1:560).

Montague Toplady (1740–78) described the London divine not long after his death.[14]

Gill's spirituality

The question of whether John Gill was a Hyper-Calvinist, namely, that he was opposed to preachers urging all and sundry to come to Christ, has dominated the way that Gill has been remembered.[15] As a result, other crucial elements of his legacy has been forgotten, among them Gill's spirituality.[16] Richard Muller, for example, in a fine examination of certain aspects of Gill's Trinitarianism, argues that "Gill's precise systematization … of Christian theology" lacked "the warm piety of earlier Reformed and

---

[14] Augustus Montague Toplady, Letter to William Lunell, October 25, 1771 (Thomas Haweis Collection, Center for Methodist Studies Collections, Bridwell Library, Southern Methodist University).

[15] See David Mark Rathel, "John Gill and the Charge of Hyper-Calvinism: Assessing Contemporary Arguments in Defense of Gill in Light of Gill's Doctrine of Eternal Justification," *The Southern Baptist Journal of Theology* 25, no.1 (Spring 2021): 43–62.

[16] See the extremely helpful study of Gill's piety by Gregory A. Wills, "A Fire That Burns Within: The Spirituality of John Gill" in Haykin, ed., *Life and Thought of John Gill*, 191–210. Also see Oliver, *History of the English Calvinistic Baptists*, 12–15.

Puritan thought."[17] While Christopher J. Ellis, in an otherwise superb study of the history of Baptist worship, contrasts the "warm evangelical spirituality" of the West Country Particular Baptists that was centred on Bristol Baptist Academy with the dominant Hyper-Calvinist tradition of Gill in London which was accompanied, according to Ellis, by "a deep suspicion of the religious affections."[18] But the actual situation is far more complex.

An excellent entrance-point into Gill's piety is first of all found in his poignant funeral sermon for his daughter Elizabeth, who died at the age of twelve on May 30, 1738. After preaching on 1 Thessalonians 4:13–14, Gill intended to give some details about his daughter's conversion, Christian walk, and final days, but the emotion of the moment appears to have overwhelmed him and he added his remarks later.[19]

---

[17] Richard A. Muller, "The Spirit and the Covenant: John Gill's Critique of the *Pactum Salutis*," *Foundations* 24 (1981): 12.

[18] Christopher J. Ellis, *Gathering: A Theology and Spirituality of Worship in Free Church Tradition* (London: SCM Press, 2004), 32.

[19] See John Gill, *An Account of Some Choice Experiences of Elizabeth Gill* in his *A Sermon Occasioned by the Death of Elizabeth Gill* (London, 1738), 33–44. See Appendix 1 for this account.

Among the things that Gill especially noted about his daughter was her "great desire after, and a wonderful esteem of the grace of humility." And to acquire such, Gill observed that his daughter would "retire into corners, to read good books, and to desire of God to give her his grace."[20] Gill believed that God did indeed answer her prayers, for, he remarked, "to the last she entertained a mean and low opinion of her self."[21] In his *Body of Divinity* Gill noted, in the section on humility, that humility entails, among other things, "a man's thinking meanly and the worst of himself."[22] He may well have been thinking of his daughter when he wrote this. For Gill went on to say, "pride is the devil's livery; but humility is the clothing of the servants of Christ, the badge by which they are known."[23]

This stress on the importance of humility in the Christian life connects Gill to a much larger Christian tradition of spirituality that goes back to such early Christian authors as Basil of

---

[20] Gill, *Account of Some Choice Experiences*, 38–39.

[21] Gill, *Account of Some Choice Experiences*, 39.

[22] John Gill, *A Body of Practical Divinity* 1.14 (1839, Paris, AR: The Baptist Standard Bearer, 1989), 801.

[23] Gill, *Practical Divinity* 1.14, 804.

Ceasarea (*c*.330–379) and his sermon *Of humility*,[24] or the emphasis by Augustine (354–430) that ultimately the City of God is a holy community that lives by faith, hope, and self-denying love, and is thus marked by humility and obedience to God.[25] But the major source of Gill's piety was, after Scripture, Puritan divinity. Evidence of this can be found especially in his early treatise on the Song of Songs, but also at various points throughout his voluminous corpus. For example, he himself practised and also recommended to his readers and hearers the Puritan discipline of meditation, which, when it forms a regular part of a believer's walk with God, will, according to Gill, "sweetly ravish our souls, raise our affections, inflame our love, and quicken our faith."[26] As he explained further:

> By meditation a soul feeds on Christ, on his person, blood, and righteousness; and

---

[24] For a study of this sermon, see Michael A.G. Haykin, "'Strive for Glory with God': Some Reflections by Basil of Caesarea on Humility," *The Gospel Witness* 82, no.3 (September 2003): 3–6.

[25] Augustine, *City of God* 19.23.

[26] John Gill, *An Exposition of the Book of Solomon's Song, Commonly called Canticles* (London: Aaron Ward, 1728), 32 (commentary on Song of Songs 1:4).

> finds a pleasure, a sweetness, and a delight therein; ... by it a believing soul feeds upon the gospel, its truths, and promises, and receives much refreshment from thence; ... being cleansed in some measure from their former filthiness and uncleanness of their minds, they ascend heavenwards in their thoughts, desires, and affections, which they employ by meditating upon pure, spiritual, and heavenly things; ... Meditation fits a man for prayer, and fills him with praise.[27]

Gill's works would have helped, therefore, to nourish elements of a vital piety among Particular Baptists even when other areas of their communal life were in disarray. Above all, what Gill said early on in his ministry shaped the entirety of his piety, as the selections in this book reveal: "I would not willingly say or write anything that is contrary to the purity and holiness of God."[28]

---

[27] Gill, *Solomon's Song*, 171 (commentary on Song of Songs 4:2).
[28] John Gill, *The Doctrines of God's Everlasting Love to his Elect, and their Eternal Union with Christ*, 3rd ed. (London, 1752), 41.

A note on the selections

In the selections of Gill's spirituality, we have placed biblical citations in footnotes, obscure words have been replaced (in such cases, the original words of Gill have been placed in footnotes), and there have been minor modernizations of punctuation and capitalization. We have also supplied the titles for each selection. The editors would also like to thank Dr Jonathan Swan for his help in selecting some of the quotations dealing with the Trinity. In this introduction, kind permission has been granted to use portions of Michael A.G. Haykin, "Remembering Baptist Heroes: The Example of John Gill," *The Southern Baptist Journal of Theology* 25, no.1 (Spring 2021): 9–28.

Chronology

1697
November 23—John Gill is born in Kettering,
Northamptonshire, to Edward
and Elizabeth Gill.

1708
End of formal schooling.

1709
Heard a sermon from his pastor,
William Wallis, which led to his conversion.

1716
November 1—Made a public profession of faith
and was baptized.

1718
Pastoral work as an intern under John Davis at
Higham Ferrers.

1718
Married Elizabeth Negus, a member of the
Higham Ferrers church.

1719

September 20—Accepted a call by the
Particular Baptist church at Goat Yard Chapel,
Horselydown, Southwark, London.

1720

March 22—Ordained as pastor.

1724

Began sermon expositions of
the Song of Solomon.

1724

First publication: A sermon on the death of
John Smith, a deacon at his church.

1726

Publication of the pamphlet *The Ancient Mode
of Baptism by Immersion*.

1728

Publication of
Exposition of the Song of Solomon.

1731

Publication of
*The Doctrine of the Trinity
Stated and Vindicated.*

1732-1733

Preached and published a discourse on prayer and one on the singing of Psalms.[1]

1735-1738

Publication of *The Cause of God and Truth* (4 Parts), a defense of Calvinism and a reply to Daniel Whitby's *Five Points,* a well-known Arminian work.

1738

May 30, 1738—Death of Gill's daughter, Elizabeth.

1746-1748

Publication of *An Exposition of the New Testament* (3 volumes).

---

[1] See selections 27 and 28.

1748

Granted a degree of Doctor of Divinity from Marischal College at the University of Aberdeen.

1748-1766

Publication of *An Exposition of the Old Testament* (6 volumes).

1752

Published *The Doctrine of the Saints' Final Perseverance* in answer to pamphlets by John Wesley.

1757

October 9—The official opening of the newly-erected church building in Carter-Lane, near London Bridge, in Southwark.

1764

October 10—Death of Gill's wife.

1767

Publication of *A Dissertation on the Antiquity of the Hebrew Language*.

1769

Publication of *A Body of Doctrinal Divinity*
in two volumes.

1770

Publication of *A Body of Practical Divinity*
in one volume.

1771

October 14—John Gill died and was buried
with other Dissenters in Bunhill-Fields,
London.

1

The satisfaction of Christ[1]

The finishing and making an entire end of sin—this was Christ's work assigned him in covenant and asserted in prophecy. And which was done when he made reconciliation or atonement for sin.[2] Not that the being of sin was removed thereby, for that remains in all the justified and sanctified ones in this life, but the damning power of it [was removed]. Those for whom[3] Christ has made satisfaction shall never come into condemnation nor be hurt by the second death: it[4] shall have no power over them.

Sin is so done and put away and abolished by the sacrifice of Christ for it that no charge can ever be brought against his people for it. The curse of the law cannot reach them, nor light

---

[1] From John Gill, *A Body of Doctrinal and Practical Divinity* 1.5 (London: Thomas Tegg, 1839), 2:46–47.
[2] Daniel 9:24.
[3] Original: Such for Christ.
[4] Original: that shall.

upon them. Nor any sentence of condemnation and death can be executed on them. Nor any punishment inflicted on them. They are secure from wrath to come.

Sin is so finished and made an end of by Christ's satisfaction for it that it will be seen no more by the eye of avenging justice. It is so put away and out of sight that when it is sought for, it shall not be found. God, for Christ's sake, has cast it behind his back and into the depths of the sea.[5]

---

[5] Micah 7:19.

2
The resurrection of the body[1]

This doctrine appears to be of great importance and usefulness, and therefore to be abode by. It is one of the articles of the creed of the ancient Jews; it is reckoned among the first principles of the doctrine of Christ; it is a fundamental article of the Christian faith. The resurrection of Christ stands and falls with it; the whole gospel is connected with it, and depends on it,[2] without this, there is no expectation of a future and better state,[3] practical religion greatly depends on the truth and belief of it.

It has been observed,[4] that the opposers of it have always had bad lives; it is a natural

---

[1] From John Gill, *A Body of Doctrinal and Practical Divinity* 2.4 (London: Thomas Tegg, 1839), 2:229.
[2] 1 Corinthians 15:13–17.
[3] 1 Corinthians 15:18–19.
[4] Gill refers to a passage from Tertullian's *On the resurrection of the flesh* 11: "For no man lives so carnally as those who deny a carnal resurrection."

consequence, what the apostle observes of the denial of it.[5] Whereas, a firm belief of it promotes a studious concern of a holy life and conversation as may he observed in the experience and practice of the apostle Paul.[6] It is very useful to instruct in various things: it serves to enlarge our views of the divine perfections; as of the omnipotence and omniscience of God, of his holiness and justice, of his immutability in his counsels and purposes, and of his faithfulness in his promises and threatenings.

It teaches us to think highly of Christ, as God over all, and as possessed of all divine perfection, since he has so great a concern in it; and serves to endear the Spirit of God, and teach us not to grieve him, by whom we are sealed to the day of the redemption of our bodies. And it may be a means of encouraging our faith and trust in God, in the greatest straits and difficulties, as being able to deliver out of them.[7] And it may direct us to a due and proper care of our bodies, while living, that they are not abused through avarice or intemperance; and to provide or give

---

[5] 1 Corinthians 15:32.
[6] Acts 24:15–16.
[7] Romans 4:16; 2 Corinthians 1:9–10.

orders for the decent interment of them after death.

This doctrine affords much comfort; hence, in the Syriac version of John 11:24 it is called, "the consolation at the last day." It may be of great use to support saints under the loss of near relations,[8] under their various trials and afflictions, under present diseases and disorders of body—from all [of] which they will be freed at the resurrection—and in the views of death, and of the changes the body will undergo after death. And yet, [our belief in this doctrine gives us confidence that we will] after all rise again, and see God, and enjoy the company of angels and saints.[9]

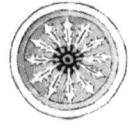

---

[8] 1 Thessalonians 4:13–14.
[9] Job 19:26–27.

3
Applying unto God for mercy[1]

"Have mercy upon me, O God"
(Psalm 51:1)

David, under a sense of sin, does not run away from God, but applies unto him and casts himself at his feet and upon his mercy; which shows the view he had of his miserable condition, and that he saw there was mercy in God. This gave him hope, and upon his bended knees and in the exercise of faith, he asks for [mercy] …

"According to thy loving-kindness"
(Psalm 51:1)

Not according to his merits, nor according to the general mercy of God—which carnal men rely upon—but according to his everlasting and unchangeable love in Christ. From which as the source, and through whom as the medium,

---

[1] John Gill, *Exposition of the Old & New Testaments* (1810, Paris, AR: The Baptist Standard Bearer, 1989), 3:738 (From John Gill commentary on Psalm 51:1).

special mercy comes to the children of men. The acts of special mercy are according to the sovereign will of God. He is not moved to mercy neither by the merits nor misery of men, but by his free grace and favour. It is love that sets mercy to work: this is a most glaring gleam of Gospel light, which none of the inspired writers... except [for] the Apostle Paul saw...

"According unto the multitude of thy tender mercies blot out my transgressions" (Ps. 51:1)

For his sin was complicated, attended with many others; and, besides, upon a view of this, he was led to observe all his other sins; and particularly the corruption of his nature, his original sin, which he mentions in verse 5 of this Psalm.[2] These he desires might be "blotted out;" out of the book of account, out of God's debt book. [He desires] that they might not stand against him, being debts he was not able to pay or make satisfaction for. And out of the tablets of his own heart and conscience—where they were ever before him and seemed to be engraven—that they might be caused to pass from him and he might

---

[2] Original: which he mentions Psalms 51:5.

have no more conscience of them. He desires that they might be blotted out as a cloud by the clear shining of the sun of righteousness, with the healing of pardoning grace in his wings; that they might be wiped away … and all this "according to the multitude of [his] tender mercies."

The mercy of God is plenteous and abundant. He is rich in it, and various are the instances of it. And it is exceedingly tender, like that of a father to his children, or like that of a mother to the son of her womb, and from this abundant and tender mercy springs the forgiveness of sin.[3] The psalmist makes mention of the multitude of the mercies of God, because of the multitude of his sins, which required a multitude of mercy to forgive, and to encourage his hope of it.

---

[3] Luke 1:77.

4

The blessedness of those who have imputed righteousness[1]

Consider the blessedness of those persons who have this righteousness imputed to them. They are freed from all sin and condemnation: not from the being of sin, but from the guilt of it and all obligation to punishment. For there is no condemnation to them who are in Christ Jesus,[2] to them who are made the righteousness of God, in him, they may say as the apostle did, "Who shall say anything to the charge of God's elect? It is God that justifies, who shall condemn; it is Christ that died."[3] And therefore they must be happy persons, for blessed is the man whose iniquities are forgiven, and whose sin is covered;

---

[1] From John Gill, *The Doctrine of Imputed Righteousness Without Works Asserted And Proved* ([London,] 1784), 23–24.

[2] Romans 8:1.

[3] Romans 8:33, 34.

blessed is the man to whom the Lord will not impute sin.[4] ...

Their persons and services are both acceptable to God, he is well pleased with both for Christ's righteousness sake. Christ's garments smell of myrrh, aloes and cassia, with which his people being clad, the Lord smells a sweet smell in them, as the smell of a field which the Lord hath blessed. Their persons come up with acceptance before him, and their sacrifices both of prayer and praise are grateful to him through the person, blood, righteousness and mediation of Christ's righteousness which is imputed to them. [This] shall never be taken away from them, [and] is one of those blessings he will never reverse, and one of those gifts of his which are without repentance.

It shall go well with these persons in life, at death, and at judgment: "Say ye to the righteous, that it shall be well with him."[5] It shall go well with him in life, for all things work together for his good.[6] It shall go well with him at death, for the righteous hath hope in his death, founded

---

[4] Psalm 32:1.
[5] Isaiah 3:10. Originally paraphrased slightly, here reproduced from the KJV exactly.
[6] See Romans 8:28.

upon this righteousness imputed to him. It shall go well with him at judgment, for this righteousness will answer for him at that time and bring him off clear at God's courts[7] and introduce him into his kingdom and glory.

Such persons are heirs of glory and shall everlastingly enjoy it, for being justified by grace, they are made heirs according to the hope of eternal life.[8] Justification and glorification are closely connected together. For whom God justified, them he also glorified.[9] Justified persons may comfortably argue from their justification to their glorification, and strongly conclude with the apostle that if they are justified by the blood of Christ, they shall be saved from wrath through him.[10] I shall add no more, but some short improvement of what has been said.

1. Seek first the kingdom of God and his righteousness, for without a righteousness there will be no admittance into heaven. And such a righteousness must be commensurate[11] to all the

---

[7] Original: bars.
[8] See Titus 3:7.
[9] See Romans 8:30.
[10] See Romans 5:9.
[11] Original: such a one it must be, as is commensurate.

demands of God's righteous law, for no other will be satisfactory to divine justice.

2. Go to Christ for such a one, in whom only it is to be had, who is the end of the law for righteousness, to every one that believes,[12] it may be had in him, it cannot be had in any other. For surely, or only, shall one say, in the Lord have I righteousness and strength.[13]

3. Admire the grace of God, in imputing this righteousness to you, and rejoice therein; it is grace in Christ: to procure, and grace in the Father to impute it, and grace in the Spirit to apply it. Admire the grace of each person herein, and ascribe the glory of your justification to it.

4. Miserable will those persons be, who will be found at the last day without this righteousness, for such shall not inherit the kingdom of God, they will not be admitted into the wedding chamber, not having on the wedding garment, but orders will be given to bind them hand and feet, and cast them into outer darkness, where will be weeping, wailing and gnashing of teeth.

---

[12] See Romans 10:4.
[13] See Isaiah 45:24.

5
The Gospel[1]

The gospel is from heaven. It is good news from a far country, which far country is heaven. The gospel is, with the Holy Ghost, sent down from heaven.[2] And Christ that spoke it, is he that speaketh from heaven.[3] The question put concerning the baptism of John, "Whence was it? from heaven, or of men?" may be put concerning the gospel and answered as such: that it is from heaven, and not of men.[4] It comes from God: Father, Son, and Spirit; from God the Father, and is therefore called the gospel of God, that is, [of] the Father, concerning his Son Jesus Christ.[5] He ordained the gospel[6] before the world was and in time committed [it] into the

---

[1] From John Gill, *A Body of Doctrinal and Practical Divinity* 4.7 (London: Thomas Tegg, 1839), 1:532–533.

[2] 1 Peter 1:12.

[3] Hebrews 12:25.

[4] Matthew 21:25.

[5] Romans 1:1, 3.

[6] Original: Which he ordained.

hands of men to preach, whom he made and makes able ministers of it and which he blesses and succeeds.

It comes also from Christ, the Son of God, and is called, the gospel of his Son, the gospel of Christ, the word of Christ, and the testimony of our Lord.[7] Christ is the subject, sum, and substance of it, as well as the author, even his person, offices, and grace, and of which he was the preacher when here on earth. For this preaching[8] he was qualified by the Spirit without measure, and spoke and preached it as never man did; and by whom it was revealed and brought to light in the clearest manner—hence the apostle says, he received it "by the revelation of Jesus Christ."[9]

The gospel[10] may be said likewise to come from the Holy Spirit of God, the inditer[11] of the Scriptures, wherein it lies. The Spirit searches the deep things of it and reveals them to men; and leads the ministers of it into all the truths

---

[7] Romans 1:9, 16; Colossians 3:16; 2 Titus 1:8.
[8] Original: For which.
[9] Galatians 1:12.
[10] Original: It
[11] Middle English word meaning "writer" or "composer."

thereof and makes their ministrations of it powerful and successful. And by the gospel,[12] he and his grace, comparable to the golden oil, are conveyed and received into the hearts of men.

The instruments of declaring, publishing, and proclaiming the gospel and its truths to the children of men are the prophets of the Old Testament who made a report of it, though believed but by few; the angels who descended at the birth of Christ and brought the good news of it; John the Baptist, the forerunner of Christ, who pointed him out as the Son of God and as the Lamb of God that took away the sin of the world; the apostles of Christ who had a commission from him to preach the gospel to every creature; and all ordinary ministers of the Word whose business it is to publish good tidings of good things.

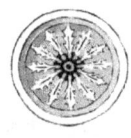

---

[12] Original: And whereby.

6
Sanctification[1]

Sanctification is absolutely necessary to salvation. It is necessary for many things. It is necessary to the saints as an evidence of their election and redemption. This is the closing work of grace and is the evidence of all that goes before. It is necessary to church fellowship, to the communion of saints in a social manner. Members of churches are described as holy brethren, saints, and faithful in Christ Jesus, and none are meet to be admitted among them but such who are so, for "what fellowship hath righteousness with unrighteousness?"[2]

Sanctification is necessary as a meetness[3] for heaven, for the inheritance of the saints in light. Without regeneration, in which sanctification is

---

[1] From John Gill, *A Body of Doctrinal and Practical Divinity* 1.14 (London: Thomas Tegg, 1839), 2:151.

[2] 2 Corinthians 6:14–16.

[3] By "meetness," Gill has in mind a fitness or a suitableness.

begun, no man shall see, nor enter, into the kingdom of God. It is absolutely necessary for the beatific vision of God in a future state—"Without holiness no man shall see the Lord"—but being possessed of that, shall see him and enjoy uninterrupted communion with him forever.[4]

To say no more, it is necessary for the work of heaven, which is singing songs of praise—songs of electing, redeeming, regenerating, calling, and persevering grace. How can unholy persons join with the saints in such work and service as this? Yea, it would be irksome and disagreeable to themselves, could they be admitted to it, and were capable of it. Neither of which can be allowed.

---

[4] Hebrews 12:14; Matthew 5:8; Psalm 17:15.

7
Of communion with God[1]

Communion is founded in union and arises from it. There is a union between God and his people. [And it is] for the more open manifestation and evidence of this that our Lord prays, "That they all may be one, as thou, Father, art in me, and I in thee, that they also may be one in us."[2] This original union is a federal union between God and them, taking them into a covenant relation to himself; by virtue of which he becomes their God, and they become his people. It is a conjugal union between them, as between husband and wife; "thy Maker is thine Husband."[3]

The evidence of this union is the gift of the Spirit to them in regeneration and conversion, when there appears to be a vital union and a

---

[1] From John Gill, *A Body of Doctrinal and Practical Divinity* 3.24 (London: Thomas Tegg, 1839), 2:552.
[2] John 17:21.
[3] Isaiah 54:5.

mutual inhabitation of God in them, and of them in God: "hereby we know that we dwell in him, and he in us, because he hath given us of his Spirit."[4]

The bond of this union is the everlasting love of God to them. As it is the love of one friend to another which knits their souls together—as the soul of Jonathan was knit to the soul of David, and Jonathan loved him as his own soul[5]—and as the saints in a spiritual relation are "knit together in love"[6] and by it, [for] love is the cement which unites them, so it is the love of God in his heart towards his people which attracts them to him and unites them with him.

And this bond is indissoluble, for nothing shall be able to "separate from the love of God,"[7] nor to separate from him [those] who are claimed in[8] his love. And in the manifestation of this love unto them lies much of their experienced[9] communion with God. As an effect and evidence of this, his everlasting love to them, he

---

[4] 1 John 4:13.
[5] See 1 Samuel 18:1.
[6] Colossians 2:2.
[7] Romans 8:39.
[8] Original: interested in.
[9] Original: sensible communion.

with lovingkindness draws them to himself in the effectual calling—when large displays are made of it to them, and at times they have some plentiful effusions of it.

The love of God is shed abroad in their hearts by the Spirit that is given them, and their hearts are directed into the love of God—insomuch that they are "rooted and grounded"[10] in it, and are persuaded of their interest in it—and comprehend, with all saints, what is the breadth, and length, and depth, and height of it.[11] They are made to drink largely of this river of pleasure… in the participation of which they have much solace and refreshment, and enjoy much communion with God. [...]

It is a wonderful instance of condescension in God; that he who is the high and lofty One, who dwells in heaven, the high and holy place, and yet with such also who are of a contrite and humble spirit; that he whose throne the heaven is, and the earth his footstool, and yet condescends to dwell with men on earth; that Wisdom, or the Son of God, should build a house, furnish a table, and invite sinful unworthy

---

[10] Ephesians 3:17.
[11] See Ephesians 3:17–18.

creatures to partake of the entertainments of it; that Father, Son, and Spirit should come and make their abode with sinful men, and admit them to the greatest intimacy with them.

It is very honorable to the sons of men to be favored with such communion: if it was an honour to Mephibosheth to sit at the table of king David, as one of the king's sons; or for Haman to be invited to a banquet with the king and queen; how infinitely more honorable is it to be admitted to sit with the King of kings at his table, and be entertained by him as royal guests!

This is a privilege very desirable, nothing more so; this is the one thing saints are desirous of in public worship, to behold the beauty of the Lord; to see his power and his glory in his sanctuary; to sit under his shadow, and taste his pleasant fruits. This is no other than the gate of heaven.

It is exceeding valuable; it is beyond all the enjoyments of life, preferable to everything that can be had on earth; the light of God's countenance, his gracious presence, communion with him, put more joy and gladness into the hearts of his people, than the greatest increase of worldly things; it is this which makes wisdom's ways of pleasantness, and her paths of peace; it is this which makes the tabernacles of God amiable and lovely, and a day in his house better than a thousand elsewhere; and because so valuable, hence the apostle John, in an exulting manner, says, "Truly, our fellowship is with the Father, and with his Son Jesus Christ!"[12]

[12] 1 John 1:3.

DR. GILL'S PULPIT.

8
Of the public ministry of the Word[1]

In general, [the ministry of the Word] is for the enlargement of the interest of Christ in the world; and it is by means of the gospel being preached to all nations in all the world that the kingdom of Christ has been spread everywhere. Not only in Judea, where the gospel was first preached, but throughout the Gentile world, multitudes were converted and churches were set up everywhere, Christianity triumphed, and heathenism [was] everywhere abolished. Julian the apostate, observing this—in imitation of the Christians and thinking thereby to increase and establish heathenism—appointed lectures and expositions of heathenish dogmas, respecting both morality and things more abstruse, and

---

[1] From John Gill, *A Body of Doctrinal and Practical Divinity* 5.5 (London: Thomas Tegg, 1839), 2:671.

public prayers, and singing at stated hours, in pagan temples.[2]

The ministry of the Word is for the conversion of sinners; without which churches would not be increased nor supported, and must in course fail, and come to nothing. But the hand of the Lord being with his ministers, many in every age believe and turn to the Lord and are added to the churches; by which means they are kept up and preserved. And hence it is necessary for the ministers of the Word to set forth the lost and miserable estate and condition of men by nature, the danger they are in, the necessity of regeneration and repentance, and of a better righteousness than their own, and of faith in Christ. These things are blessed for the turning of men from darkness to light, and from the power of Satan unto God.

---

[2] Gill inserts a footnote here, citing two sources: Gregory of Nazianzus, *Orations 4 & 5: Invective Against Julian the Emperor*, and Sozomen, *Ecclesiastical History* 5.16.

9
Christ on the cross[1]

"My God, my God, why hast thou forsaken me?"
(Psalm 22:1)

God is the God of Christ as he is man; he prepared a body for him, a human nature; anointed it with the oil of gladness; supported it under all its sorrows and sufferings, and at last exalted it at his own right hand. And Christ behaved towards him as his covenant God; prayed to him, believed in him, loved him, and was obedient to him as such.

Here [Christ] expresses his faith of interest in him, when he hid his face from him, on account of which he protests to[2] him thus, "why hast thou forsaken me?" which is to be understood, not as if the hypostatical[3] or personal

---

[1] John Gill, *Exposition of the Old & New Testaments* (1810, Paris, AR: The Baptist Standard Bearer, 1989), 3:616 (commentary on Psalm 22:1).

[2] Original: expostulates with him.

[3] The hypostatic union is a theological term meaning the unity of the two natures (divine and human) of Jesus Christ in his person.

union of the divine and human natures were dissolved, or that the one was now separated from the other: for the fulness of the Godhead still dwelt bodily in him. Nor that he ceased to be the object of the Father's love; for so he was in the midst of all his sufferings—yea, his Father loved him because he laid down his life for the sheep. Nor that the principle of joy and comfort was lost in him, [but] only the act and sense of it. He was now deprived of the gracious presence of God, of the manifestations of his love to his human soul, and had a sense[4] of divine wrath, not for his own sins, but for the sins of his people, and was for a while destitute of help and comfort.

All of this was necessary in order to make satisfaction for sin; for as he had the sins of his people imputed to him, he must bear the whole punishment of them, which is twofold: the punishment of loss and the punishment of sense. The former lies in a deprivation of the divine presence, and the latter in a sense of divine

---

[4] Here, and in the next paragraph, Gill is using the word "sense" to mean "an experience of."

wrath, and both Christ sustained as the surety[5] of his people.

This expostulation[6] is made not as ignorant of the reason of it—he knew that as he was wounded and bruised for the sins of his people, he was deserted on the same account—nor as impatient, for he was a mirror of patience in all his sufferings; and much less as in despair; for, in these very words, he strongly expresses and repeats his faith of interest in God.[7]

But this is done to set forth the greatness and bitterness of his sufferings; that not only men hid their faces from him, and the sun in the firmament withdrew its light and heat from him, but what was most grievous of all: his God departed from him. From hence it appears that he was truly man, had a human soul, and endured sorrows and sufferings in it. And this may be of use to Christians,[8] to expect the hidings of God's face, though on another account; and to teach them to wait patiently for him, and to trust in

---

[5] A surety is a person who accepts legal responsibility for another person.

[6] An expostulation is a remonstrance or protest. Here Gill is referring to the words of Christ, "My God, my God, why hast thou forsaken me?"

[7] See Psalms 22:8 and Isaiah 50:6.

[8] Original: to his members.

the Lord, and stay themselves upon their God, even while they walk in darkness and see no light.

10
The Church as the "rose of Sharon"[9]

"I am the rose of Sharon"
(Song of Solomon 2:1)

The church may be compared to "the rose" [in four ways].

1. Beauty. It is called the beautiful flower—its colour is beautiful and delightful. The comparison[10] is exceedingly just, [for] nothing is more common in poems of this kind than to set forth the beauty of women by the rose. ... The church may be fitly compared to it. No "rose of Sharon" can be more beautiful in colour and delightful to the eye than the church is in the eyes of Christ, as she is clothed with his pure and spotless righteousness, adorned with the graces of his Spirit, and standing at his right-hand in cloth of gold, bespangled with the sparkling gems of divine grace. Her beauty is desirable to

---

[9] From John Gill, *An Exposition of the Book of Solomon's Song* (London: William Hill Collingridge, 1854), 66.

[10] Original: figure.

him, she being in his eye "the fairest among women."[11]

2. Its sweet odor. The church and all believers are as the fragrant and sweet-smelling rose; their persons are so as considered in Christ. And [so are] all their graces—especially when in exercise—and all their duties and services when performed in faith and perfumed with Christ's mediation.[12]

3. Its delight in sunny places. It thrives and flourishes the best there and has the most fragrant smell. Christ is "the sun of righteousness,"[13] under whose warming, comforting and refreshing beams, believers delight to be, and under which their souls grow, thrive, blossom exceedingly, and bring forth much fruit.

4. Its blossoming and flourishing; "the desert shall rejoice and blossom as the rose."[14] The church may be said to do so when there is a large increase of members, and these much in the exercise of grace, and "fruitful in every good

---

[11] Song of Solomon 1:8.
[12] See Song of Solomon 4:10; Philippians 4:18; Revelation 5:8; 8:3–4.
[13] Malachi 4:2.
[14] Isaiah 35:1.

work."[15] Then may the church be said to be as the blossoming rose.

---

[15] Colossians 1:10.

Pliny the Elder

11

The Church as the lily of the valley[1]

"And the lily of the valleys"
(Song of Solomon 2:1)

Believers are trees of righteousness and plants of Christ's Father's planting. They[2] do not run along the ground and cleave to earthly things, but lift up their heads heavenwards and grow up on high in their desires and affections, having their hearts above, where their treasure is. Believers are like the flowers of the lily, open towards heaven, but shut towards the earth.

Consider[3] the weakness of its body, and largeness of its head: Pliny says of the lily that it has "a weak neck, or body, which is not sufficient

---

[1] From John Gill, *An Exposition of the Book of Solomon's Song* (London: William Hill Collingridge, 1854), 66–67.
[2] Original: which.
[3] Original: For.

to bear the weight of the head."[4] Christ is the head of the body, the church, and far greater than that; he is not supported by it, but he supports it. The church's strength lies in her head, as Samson's did in his locks. She is weak in herself, but strong in Christ her head, and therefore says, "surely in the Lord have I righteousness and strength."[5]

The church may be compared, not only to a lily, but to "a lily of the valleys." ... Valleys are low places, and when the church is called "the lily of the valleys," it may be expressive of the low estate and condition which she is sometimes in. Believers are Christ's myrtle-trees, and these are sometimes in the bottom—in a low condition—but he grants his presence with them and the discoveries of his love to them. They are his doves, and they are often "like doves of the valleys, mourning everyone for their iniquity,"[6] being humbled and pressed down in their souls under a sense of sin and unworthiness. They are not only humble in themselves, and low in their

---

[4] The original quotes the Latin in the body of the text: "languido semper collo et non sufficiente capitis oneri." The quote is taken from Pliny the Elder, *Natural History* 21.11.

[5] See Isaiah 45:24.

[6] See Ezekiel 7:16.

own eyes, but are often in the deeps of affliction, sorrow, and distress, and out of these depths cry unto the Lord.[7]

---

[7] See Psalm 130:1.

12
Christ in the lily of the valley[1]

Now Christ may be called, by way of eminency, … the chiefest and most excellent flower in the field. There is no such flower in the heavenly paradise as he is. Among all the holy angels and glorified saints, there are none to be compared with him. And in his garden here below, no such flower grows as this. He is "the flower," the choicest, the best, and the most excellent in the whole field or garden.

The flower of the field is liable to be plucked up or trodden under feet by beasts, [so likewise] Christ was exposed to the rage and fury of his enemies, those "strong bulls of Bashan" of which he complains.[2] This sweet flower was laid hold on by "wicked hands,"[3] and cropped; and still his precious person, blood, and righteousness, are

---

[1] From John Gill, *An Exposition of the Book of Solomon's Song* (London: William Hill Collingridge, 1854), 69.
[2] Psalm 22:13–14.
[3] Acts 2:23.

slighted, condemned, and "trodden under foot" by Christless and unconverted sinners.[4]

This may be expressive of the meanness of Christ in the esteem of the world: a field-flower is little regarded. Christ is as "a root out of a dry ground," and therefore they say, "he hath no form nor comeliness, and when we shall see him, there is no beauty that we should desire him: hence he is despised and rejected of men," they not knowing the real worth and value of this precious flower.[5]

The flower of the field is not of man's planting, nor is it raised by his care and industry: [so likewise] Christ was conceived in the womb of a virgin, and born of her without the help of man. Like[6] the flower of the field, he had no father but his Father in heaven, and no mother but the virgin on earth; and so was Melchizedek's antitype, "without father as man, and without mother as God."[7]

The flower of the field is open to all. Whoever will may come to Christ for life and salvation; there is liberty of access to all sorts of

---

[4] See Hebrews 10:29.
[5] See Isaiah 53:2–3.
[6] Original: As.
[7] See Hebrews 7:3.

sinners to come to him and partake of his sweetness and benefits. He is not a flower in an enclosed garden that cannot be reached,[8] but stands in the open field. Every sinner that labors under a sense of sin and is heavy laden with the weight and burden of it may come to him and not fear a rejection from him. He is not "a fountain sealed, but opened to the house of David, and inhabitants of Jerusalem, for sin and for uncleanness."[9] ...

He may be said to be the lily of the valleys because of his wonderful humility and condescension in assuming our nature, suffering in our stead, and in humbling himself unto the death of the cross for us. His whole life was one continued series of humility, as was his death an undeniable instance of it: Christ here on earth did not appear as the lofty cedar, but as the lowly lily; and that not of the mountains, but of the valleys. And it is with humble souls he delights to dwell. For though he is the high and lofty one—in his divine nature—yet he condescends to dwell with such who are of a humble and contrite spirit.[10]

---

[8] Original: cannot be come at.
[9] See Zechariah 13:1.
[10] See Isaiah 57:15.

13
The first and chief commandment[1]

"And thou shalt love the Lord thy God"
(Deuteronomy 6:5)

This is the first and chief commandment in the law, the sum and substance of the first tablet. It includes in it—or at least has connected with it—knowledge of God, esteem of him, delight in him, faith and trust in him, fear and worship of him, and obedience to him; which when right springs from it. God is to be loved because of the perfections of his nature and the works of his hand: of nature, providence, and grace. And also[2] because of the relations he stands in to men, and especially to his own people; and because of his peculiar love to them. And, indeed, he is to be loved by all men for his care of them and blessings of goodness bestowed on them.

---

[1] From John Gill, *Exposition of the Old & New Testaments* (1810, Paris, AR: The Baptist Standard Bearer, 1989), 2:28 (commentary on Deuteronomy 6:5).

[2] Original: And because.

The manner in which this is to be done follows: "with all thine heart, and with all thy soul, and with all thy might" (Deuteronomy 6:5). With a superlative love, … with the whole of the affections of the heart, with great fervency and ardour of spirit, in the sincerity of the soul, and with all the strength of grace a man has; with such love that is as strong as death.[3]

---

[3] See Song of Solomon 8:6.

14
Bless the Lord, O my soul[1]

"Bless the Lord, O my soul"
(Psalm 103:1)

[The psalmist speaks of] his better part—his soul—which comes immediately from God and returns to him, which is immaterial and immortal and of more worth than the world. God is to be served with the best we have: as with the best of our substance, so with the best of our persons. And it is the heart, or soul, which he requires to be given him. And such service as is performed with the soul or spirit is most agreeable to him. He is a Spirit and therefore must be worshipped in spirit and in truth.[2] Unless the spirit or soul of a man is engaged in the service of God, it is of little avail—for bodily exercise profiteth not.[3]

---

[1] From John Gill, *Exposition of the Old & New Testaments* (1810, Paris, AR: The Baptist Standard Bearer, 1989), 4:132–133 (commentary on Psalm 103:1–2).

[2] See John 4:24.

[3] See 1 Timothy 4:8.

Preaching, hearing, praying, and praising should be with both the spirit and with the understanding. Here the psalmist calls upon his soul to "bless" the Lord, not by invoking or conferring a blessing on him—which as it is impossible to be done, so he stands in no need of it, being God all sufficient and blessed for evermore—but by proclaiming and congratulating his blessedness and by giving him thanks for all mercies, spiritual and temporal.

"And all that is within me, bless his holy name"
(Psalm 103:1)

… Meaning not only all within his body—his heart, kidneys,[4] lungs, etc.—but all within his soul: all the powers and faculties of it. His understanding, will, affections, and judgment; and all the grace that was wrought in him: faith, hope, love, joy, and the like. These he would have all involved[5] and employed in praising the name of the Lord which is exalted above all blessing and praise [and] is great and glorious in all the earth by reason of his works wrought and

---

[4] Original: reins.
[5] Original: concerned.

blessings of goodness bestowed. And that name[6] appears to be holy in them all, as it does in the works of creation, providence, and redemption. At the remembrance of that holiness thanks should be given, for he that is glorious in holiness is fearful in praises.[7]

"Bless the Lord, O my soul, and forget not all his benefits"

This phrase[8] is repeated to show the importance of the service, and the vehement desire of the psalmist that his soul should be engaged in it. Not any of [his benefits]; the least of them are not to be forgotten, being such as men are altogether unworthy of. They flow not from the merit of men, but from the mercy of God. And they are many, even innumerable. They are new every morning and continue all the day. And how great must the sum of them be—not one should be forgotten—and yet even good men are very apt to forget them, as the Israelites of old who sung the praises of the Lord soon forgot his works.

---

[6] Original: and which.
[7] Psalm 97:12.
[8] Original: Which is.

The Lord, knowing the weakness of his people's memories, has not only, under the Gospel dispensation, appointed an ordinance to be continued to the end of the world to commemorate a principal blessing and benefit of his—redemption by his Son—but has also promised his Spirit to bring all things to their remembrance. And believers should remember[9] what God has done for them in order both to show gratitude and thankfulness to him and for the encouragement of their faith and hope in him.

---

[9] Original: And this believers should be concerned for: that they do remember.

15
Blessed are the merciful[1]

"Blessed are the merciful"
(Matthew 5:7)

Blessed are those who show mercy to the bodies of men, to those that are poor, indigent, and miserable in their outward circumstances; by both sympathizing with them and distributing unto them, not only making use of expressions of pity and concern but communicating with readiness and cheerfulness, affection and tenderness, and with a view to the glory of God.

Blessed are those who also show mercy to the souls of men, by instructing such as are ignorant, giving them good counsel and advice: reproving them for sin, praying for them, forgiving injuries done by them, and by comforting those that are cast down. To show mercy is very delightful to and desirable by God. It is what he requires, and is one of the weightier matters of

---

[1] From John Gill, *Exposition of the Old & New Testaments* (1809, Paris, AR: The Baptist Standard Bearer, 1989), 7:38 (commentary on Matthew 5:7).

the law. It is very ornamental[2] to a child of God, and makes him more like to his heavenly Father. ...

> *"They shall obtain mercy"*
> *(Matthew 5:7)*

... Men are said to obtain this [mercy] when they are regenerated and called by grace; and when they have a discovery—and an application—of the forgiveness of their sins. But here it seems to refer to[3] those supplies of grace and mercy which merciful persons may expect to find and obtain at the throne of grace to help them in time of need. And these shall not only obtain mercy of God in this life, but in the world to come, in the great day of the Lord.

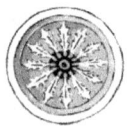

---

[2] Gill means that to show mercy in these ways adorns the believer's life and makes it beautiful.
[3] Original: design.

A

Body of Doctrinal Divinity;

OR, A

SYSTEM OF EVANGELICAL TRUTHS,

Deduced from the

SACRED SCRIPTURES.

IN TWO VOLUMES.

By *JOHN GILL*, D.D.

VOLUME I.

LONDON:
Printed for the AUTHOR,
And Sold by GEORGE KEITH, in Gracechurch - Street.
M.DCC.LXIX.

16
Seeing the beauty of God[1]

"Blessed are the pure in heart"
(Matthew 5:8)

… The heart of man is naturally unclean and it is not in the power of man to make it clean, or to be pure from his sin; nor is any man in this life, in such sense, so pure in heart as to be entirely free from sin. This is only true of Christ, angels, and glorified saints. But such may be said to be so, who—though they have sin dwelling in them—are justified from all sin by the righteousness of Christ, and are "clean through the word," or sentence of justification pronounced upon them, on the account of that righteousness.[2] [The justified are those] whose iniquities are all forgiven, and whose hearts are sprinkled with the blood of Jesus which cleanses from all sin; and who have the grace of God wrought in

---

[1] From John Gill, *Exposition of the Old & New Testaments* (1809, Paris, AR: The Baptist Standard Bearer, 1989), 7:39 (commentary on Matthew 5:8).

[2] See John 15:3.

their hearts, which, though as yet imperfect, it is entirely pure. There is not the least spot or stain of sin in it, and such souls as they are in love with, so they most earnestly desire after more purity of heart, lip, life, and conversation. ...

> *"For they shall see God"*
> *(Matthew 5:8)*

They shall see God in this life, enjoying communion with him both in private and public, in the several duties of religion, in the house and ordinances of God where they often behold his beauty, see his power and his glory, and taste and know that he is good and gracious. And [they shall see God] in the other world, where they shall see God in Christ with the eyes of their understanding, and God incarnate with the eyes of their bodies after the resurrection. This sight of Christ—and God in Christ—will be unspeakably glorious, desirable, delightful, and satisfying. It will be free from all darkness and error and from all interruption; it will be an appropriating and transforming one, and will last forever.

17
How angels serve believers[1]

[Angels] are useful in comforting the saints when in distress, as they strengthened and comforted Christ in his human nature when he was in agony. So they comfort his people,[2] as Daniel when [he was] in great terror,[3] and the apostle Paul in a tempest,[4] and as when in temporal, so when in spiritual distresses. For if evil angels are capable of suggesting terrible and uncomfortable things, and of filling the mind with blasphemous thoughts and frightful apprehensions, good angels are surely capable of suggesting comfortable things and what may relieve souls distressed with unbelief, doubts, and fears, and the temptations of Satan.

---

[1] From John Gill, *A Body of Doctrinal and Practical Divinity* 3.2 (London: Thomas Tegg, 1839), 1:383.
[2] Original: members.
[3] Daniel 9:23; 10:11, 19.
[4] Acts 27:23–24.

They are great assistants[5] in repelling the temptations of Satan. For if they oppose themselves to and have conflicts with evil angels with respect to things political and civil—the affairs of kingdoms and states in which the interest and church of Christ are concerned—they, no doubt, bestir themselves in opposition to evil spirits when they tempt believers to sin, or to despair. Angels then[6] are better able to wrestle against principalities and powers, against the rulers of the darkness of this world, and against spiritual wickednesses in high places.[7]

[Angels] are exceedingly useful to saints in their dying moments. They attend the saints on their dying beds and whisper comfortable things to them against the fears of death. They keep off the fiends of Hell from disturbing and distressing them, and they watch the moment when soul and body are parted, and carry their souls to Heaven as they carried the soul of Lazarus into Abraham's bosom.[8]

---

[5] Original: greatly assisting.
[6] Original: So that they are.
[7] Ephesians 6:12; Zechariah 3:1–4.
[8] Luke 16:22.

18

The Trinity transforms our worship, prayer, and unity[1]

The ... unity of the divine Being is of great importance in religion—especially in the affair of worship. God, the one only God, is the object of it. This is the sense of the first and second commandments, which forbid having[2] any other God but one, and the worship of any creature whatever: angels, men, or any other creature and the likeness of them. To do [so] is to worship the creature along with the Creator. But this does not mean the Son and Spirit may not have acts[3] of worship performed to them equally as to the Father; and for this reason: because they are with him the one God. Hence baptism is administered equally in the name of all Three, and

---

[1] From John Gill, *A Body of Doctrinal and Practical Divinity* 1.28 (London: Thomas Tegg, 1839), 1:186.
[2] Original: owning.
[3] Original: this hinders not but that the Son and Spirit may have acts.

prayer is jointly made unto them; both solemn acts of religious worship.[4]

And this doctrine of the unity of the divine Being—as it fixes and settles the object of worship, so being closely attended to—guides the mind right in the consideration of it while worshipping, without any confusion and division in it. Let the direction or address be to which person it may, as each may be distinctly addressed. [If] it be to the Father, he is considered in the act of worship as the one God with the Son and Spirit. If the address is to the Son, he is considered as the one God with the Father and the Spirit. Or if the address is to the Spirit, he is considered as the one God with the Father and Son.

This doctrine also serves to fix and settle the object of our faith, hope, and love without division and distraction of mind. Our faith, hope, and love[5] are not to be exercised on different objects and to be divided between them, but are to centre in one object, the one only true God: Father, Son, and Spirit; whom alone we are to make our confidence, our hope, and the centre of our affections.[6]

---

[4] See Matthew 28:19; Revelation 1:4–5.
[5] Original: which are not.
[6] Jeremiah 17:7; Psalm 73:25.

This truth—the unity of God—also[7] carries a strong and powerful argument to promote unity, harmony, and concord among the saints; for which it is used in Ephesians 4:3–6: "Endeavouring to keep the unity of the Spirit in the bond of peace. There is one body, and one Spirit, even as ye are called in one hope of your calling; One Lord, one faith, one baptism, One God and Father of all, who is above all, and through all, and in you all."[8]

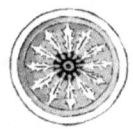

---

[7] Original: As well as this doctrine carries.

[8] The original lists the reference but does not quote the text.

19
Distinctions in the Trinity[1]

To come to the point: it is the personal relations [within the Trinity]—or distinctive relative properties which belong to each Person—which distinguish them one from another: paternity in the first Person, filiation in the second, and spiration[2] in the third. Or, more plainly, it is *begetting*[3] which peculiarly belongs to the first and is never ascribed to the second and third. This distinguishes him from them both, and gives him, with great propriety, the name of Father.

And it is being *begotten*, that is the personal relation, or relative property of the second Person; hence called "the only begotten of the

---

[1] From John Gill, *A Body of Doctrinal and Practical Divinity* 1.30 (London: Thomas Tegg, 1839), 1:203–204.

[2] From the Latin *spiratio* which means the act of breathing. Used in theology to represent "the act by or manner in which the Holy Spirit proceeds from the Father or from the Father and the Son."

[3] Psalm 2:7.

Father,"[4] which distinguishes him from the first and third, and gives him the name of the Son. And the relative property—or personal relation of the third Person—is that he is *breathed* by the first and second Persons; hence called the breath of the Almighty, the breath of the mouth of Jehovah the Father, and the breath of the mouth of Christ the Lord. And this[5] is never said of the other two Persons; and so distinguishes him from them, and very pertinently gives him the name of the Spirit, or breath.[6] ...

If one of these distinct Persons is a Father in the divine nature, and another a Son in the divine nature, there must be something in the divine nature which is the ground of the relation and distinguishes the one from the other. And [that something] can be nothing else than generation, and this distinguishes the third Person from them both, as neither begetting nor begotten. From generation arises the relation, and from relation distinct personality. And as an ancient writer[7] says, "unbegotten, begotten, and

---

[4] John 1:14.

[5] Original: which.

[6] Job 33:4; Psalm 33:6; 2 Thessalonians 2:8.

[7] Gill cites here some words from *Exposition of the True Faith*, which was attributed to Justin Martyr at the time.

proceeding," are not names of essence—and it may be added, nor of office—but are modes of subsistence; and so distinguish persons.

Upon the whole, it is easy to observe that the distinction of Persons in the Deity depends on the generation of the Son. Take away that—which would destroy the relation between the first and second Persons—and the distinction drops. And this distinction is natural and necessary—or by necessity of nature—and not arbitrary or of choice and will; if it[8] was, it might not have been at all, or have been otherwise than it is.

However, scholars now believe that it was written probably by Theodoret of Cyrus.

[8] Original: Which, if it was.

20
The Trinity is essential[1]

In the sacred writings, the economy[2] of man's salvation is clearly exhibited to us, in which we find the three divine persons, by agreement and consent, take their distinct parts. And it may be observed that the election of men to salvation is usually ascribed to the Father; redemption, or the petition[3] of salvation, to the Son; and sanctification, or the application of salvation, to the Spirit. And they are all to be met with in one passage: "Elect according to the foreknowledge of God the Father, through sanctification of the Spirit, unto obedience and sprinkling of the blood of Jesus" (1 Peter 1:2).

The same may be observed in 2 Thessalonians 2:13–14, "But we are bound to give thanks

---

[1] From John Gill, *A Body of Doctrinal and Practical Divinity* 1.30 (London: Thomas Tegg, 1839), 1:197–198, 201.

[2] The phrase "economy of salvation" is used in theological discourse to refer to God's redemptive plan.

[3] Original: impetration.

always to God for you, brethren beloved of the Lord, because God hath from the beginning chosen you to salvation through sanctification of the Spirit and belief of the truth: whereunto he called you by our gospel, to the obtaining of the glory of our Lord Jesus Christ." Here[4] God the Father is said to choose men from the beginning unto salvation, and the sanctification of the Spirit is the means through which they are chosen; and the glory of the Lord Jesus Christ the end to which they are chosen and called. But nowhere are these acts of grace more distinctly ascribed to each person than in the first chapter of the epistle to the Ephesians, where God the Father of Christ is said to bless and choose his people in him before the foundation of the world, and to predestinate them to the adoption of children by him, in whom they are accepted with him.[5] And Christ is spoken of as the author of redemption through his blood, which includes forgiveness of sin and a justifying righteousness; which entitles [Christians] to the heavenly inheritance.[6] And then the Holy Spirit—in

---

[4] Original did not cite the text of the verses, and continued with "where God the Father."

[5] Ephesians 1:3–6.

[6] Ephesians 1:7, 11.

distinction from them both—is said to be the guarantee[7] of their inheritance, and by whom they are sealed until they come to the full possession of it.[8]

The doctrine of the Trinity is often represented as a speculative point—of no great moment whether it is believed or not, too mysterious and curious to be pryed into—and that it had better be let alone than meddled with. But, alas! It enters into the whole of our salvation and all the parts of it; into all the doctrines of the gospel and into the experience of the saints. There is no doing without it. As soon as ever man is convinced of his sinful and miserable estate by nature he perceives there is a divine person that he has offended, and that there is need of another divine person to make satisfaction for his offences, and a third to sanctify him, to begin and carry on a work of grace in him, and to make him meet for eternal glory and happiness.

---

[7] Original: earnest. As found in the KJV's rendition of Ephesians 1:14.

[8] Ephesians 1:13–14.

21
Grace and truth in Christ[1]

"For the law was given by Moses"
(John 1:17)

Both moral and ceremonial [laws were given by Moses]. The moral law was given to Adam in innocence, which, having been broken—and almost lost out of the minds and memories of men—was given by Moses in a new edition of it in writing. It points out what is man's duty both to God and men, discovers sin, accuses of it, convicts of it, and condemns for it. It could not give strength to perform its demands, nor does it give the least hint of forgiveness, nor will it admit of repentance. And hence [it] is opposed to grace although[2] it was a benefit to men, being in its own nature good and useful in its effects.

The ceremonial law pointed out the pollution of human nature, the guilt and punishment

---

[1] From John Gill, *Exposition of the Old & New Testaments* (1809, Paris, AR: The Baptist Standard Bearer, 1989), 7:746 (commentary on John 1:17).

[2] Original: though.

of sin. [It] was a type and shadow of deliverance by Christ but could not give the grace it shadowed, and therefore was opposed both to grace and truth. Now both these were given by Moses to the people of the Jews, not as the maker but the minister of them. It was God who appointed each of these laws and ordained them in the hand of the mediator Moses, who received them from him by the disposition of angels and delivered them to the people of Israel. And a very high office this was he was put into, and a very great honour was conferred upon him; but Jesus Christ is a far greater person, and in a higher office:

> *"But grace and truth came by Jesus Christ"*
> *(John 1:17)*

By grace and truth is meant the Gospel, in opposition to the law. It is called grace, because it is a declaration of the love and grace of God to men. It ascribes salvation—in all the parts of it—to the free grace and favour of God, and is the means of implanting and increasing grace in the hearts of men. And the Gospel is called truth,[3] not only

---

[3] Original: And "truth."

because it contains truth, and nothing but truth—it coming from the God of truth and the substance of it being Christ, who is the truth, and being revealed, applied, and led into by the Spirit of truth—but because it is the truth of the types and the substance of the shadows of the law.

These two may mean distinct things: grace may refer to[4] all the blessings of grace which are in Christ and come by him; and truth [may refer to] the promises and the fulfilment of them, which are all yea, and amen, in Christ.[5] And when these are said to be by him, the meaning is, not that they are by him as an instrument, but as the author of them. For Christ is the author of the Gospel, the fulfiller of the promises, and the giver of all grace; which shows the superior excellency of Christ to Moses, and to all men, and even to angels also.

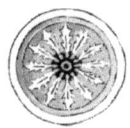

---

[4] Original: may design all.
[5] See 2 Corinthians 1:20.

22
Longing to know Christ more[1]

"That I may know him"
(Philippians 3:10)

[Paul's] knowledge of Christ, though it was very great, was imperfect. He knew but in part and therefore desired to know more of Christ, of the mystery and glories of his person, of the unsearchable riches of his grace, of his great salvation and the benefits of it, of his love which passes perfect knowledge, and to have a renewed and enlarged experience of communion with him. The apostle here explains what he means by winning Christ, for the sake of which he suffered the loss of all things and counted them but dung; it was that he might attain to a greater knowledge of the person and grace of Christ:

---

[1] From John Gill, *Exposition of the Old & New Testaments* (1809, Paris, AR: The Baptist Standard Bearer, 1989), 9:149 (commentary on Philippians 3:10).

"And the power of his resurrection"
(Philippians 3:10)

Not that power which was put forth by his Father—and by himself—in raising him from the dead; but the virtue which arises from it and the influence it has on many things, such as on the resurrection of the saints: it is the procuring cause of it—they shall rise by virtue of union to a risen Jesus. It is the firstfruits, which is the guarantee[2] and pledge of their resurrection. As sure as Christ is risen, so sure shall they rise. It is the exemplar and pattern of theirs; their bodies will be raised and fashioned like to the glorious body of Christ, and this the apostle desired to know, experience, and attain unto.

Christ's resurrection has an influence also on the justification of his people. When Christ died he had the sins of them all upon him, and he died for them, and discharged as their public head and representative, and they in him. Hence it is said of him, that "he was raised again for our justification."[3] …

---

[2] Original: the earnest.
[3] Romans 4:2.

This power and virtue the apostle had had an experience of, yet he wanted to feel more of it: in exciting the graces of the spirit to a lively exercise, in raising his affections and setting them on things above, in engaging him to seek after them and set light by things on earth, and in causing him to walk in newness of life, in likeness or imitation of Christ's resurrection, to all which that strongly animates and encourages.[4]

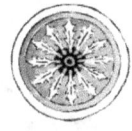

---

[4] See Colossians 3:1.

23
The presence of God[1]

For God to be with his people—and they to enjoy his presence—is for him to commune with them, as he promised to Moses that he would from off the mercy seat and to whom he granted his gracious presence in a very remarkable manner. He talked with him, as one friend does with another, in a most familiar way. So God, when with his people, affords them his gracious presence, speaks comfortable words unto them, and brings to their remembrance, and home to their souls, his gracious promises. And a word fitly spoken is like apples of gold in pictures of silver.[2] Never does a child of God experience the presence of God more than when he is pleased to bring a promise and set it home upon the heart with power.

---

[1] From John Gill, *The Presence of God, What it is, and the Means by which it May be Enjoyed* in his *Sermons and Tracts* (London: W. Hardcastle, 1814), 2:262–263.

[2] Proverbs 25:11.

For the Lord to be with his people and grant his gracious presence is to manifest his early loving kindness to their souls. Sometimes they are in darkness and see no light—God withdraws himself from them as to the manifestation of his love—though he at other times, with great kindness, gathers them by granting a fresh manifestation of his love. He may be said to be with them when he speaks to the heart and says, "I have loved thee with an everlasting love; therefore with loving kindness have I drawn thee."[3] [Or] when he sheds his love abroad in their hearts,[4] by his Spirit, or directs their hearts into his love: when they are rooted and grounded in his love, satisfied of their interest in it, and that nothing is able to separate them from it. [Or] when he enlarges their hearts to run with cheerfulness in the ways of his commandments, and draws out the desires of their souls to his name and to the remembrance of him; when he raises their affections, putting in his hand by the hole of the door, causing their "bowels to move towards him;" and their hands drop with sweet smelling myrrh, upon the handle of the lock.[5]

---

[3] Jeremiah 31:3.
[4] Romans 5:5.
[5] Song of Solomon 5:4–5.

That is, when their graces are in lively exercise when it is thus, God is with them, granting his gracious presence.

When their faith is in lively exercise; and when they can say with the church, "My Beloved is mine, and I am his;"[6] when their hope is raised to such a degree as to say, "The Lord is my portion, saith my soul, there will I hope in him."[7] When their love is so strong, as with the Psalmist to say, "I will love thee, O Lord, my God; for thou art my rock and my fortress;"[8] when they thus abound in faith, hope, and love, through the power of the Holy Ghost; then may the Lord be said to be with them, and they to enjoy his presence.

When in ordinances—particularly the hearing of the word[9]—they have a spiritual appetite, ... when there is a desire in their souls after the sincere milk of the Word, that they may grow thereby,[10] and they feed upon it and relish it; when they sit under the shadow of Christ with delight, and his fruit is sweet unto

---

[6] Song of Solomon 2:16.
[7] Lamentations 3:24.
[8] An amalgamation of Psalm 18:1 and Psalm 31:3.
[9] Original: hearing the word particularly.
[10] 1 Peter 2:2.

their taste;[11] when, while the Scriptures of truth are opened, or the Word of God preached, their hearts burn within them; then God is with them, and they enjoy his presence.

Now it is a most amazing instance of divine goodness that God should grant his gracious presence to any of the sons of men, frail, mortal creatures; sinful dust and ashes. He that dwells on high, in whom it is wonderful condescension to look on things in heaven; he, whose throne is in the heavens, and the earth is his footstool! It is a humbling of himself to look to him that is of a poor and a contrite spirit. This is grace; but how much more so for the High and the lofty One, that inhabiteth eternity, and dwells in the high and holy place, to dwell with him that is of a poor and a contrite spirit, to revive the spirit of the humble, and to revive the heart of the contrite ones![12] It is much he should look on them; but it is far more—it is amazing—that he should dwell or take up his abode with them.

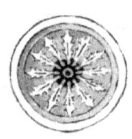

---

[11] Song of Solomon 2:3.
[12] See Isaiah 57:15; 66:2.

24
How God's presence is lost and how it is found[1]

If you forsake the Lord, for to forsake the assembling of yourselves together is to forsake him, he will forsake you. To forsake him is to forsake the throne of his grace, to restrain prayer before God; and if you continue therein, he will forsake you. You never knew a man, I dare say, in the whole circle of your acquaintance, that ever forsook the word of God and prayer, but that he was left of God (though a child of his) and manifestly appeared to be in a declining state. This is a well known case. If men forsake the Lord in either of these senses, he is sure to forsake them until he hath brought them to a sense of their evil. "I will go and return to my place, until they

---

[1] From John Gill, *The Presence of God, What it is, and the Means by which it May be Enjoyed* in his *Sermons and Tracts* (London: W. Hardcastle, 1814), 2:262–263.

acknowledge their offence, and seek my face: in their affliction they will seek me early."[2]

This forsaking of God is a very great evil which the people of God fall into through the infirmity of the flesh, the power of unbelief, the temptation of Satan and often times through being immersed in the things of this world. ... God is provoked at it and will show his displeasure. He resents it by hiding his face from them. "If ye forsake him, he will forsake you."[3]

You see then, if you are desirous of enjoying the presence of God, what is to be done. You must be with him. You must keep close to him, to the throne of his grace, to his people, to his sanctuary, and the ordinances of it. If you depart from these you are not to expect the presence of God. I am speaking of the sensible communion, which cannot be expected.

Again: What great encouragement here is to seek the Lord. "If ye seek him he will be found of you."[4] He is to be found, great as he is. He will show himself to you if ye seek him. You may be assured of it: he hath promised it.

---

[2] Hosea 5:15.
[3] 2 Chronicles 15:2.
[4] 2 Chronicles 15:2.

25
The end of all things[1]

"And he said unto me, it is done"
(Revelation 21:6)

The end of all things is come. It is all over with the first heaven and earth—these are no more—and the new heaven and earth are finished. There seems to be an allusion to the old creation: he spoke, and it was done.[2] The whole election of grace is completed. Every individual vessel of mercy is called by grace, all the saints are brought with Christ, and their bodies raised, and living saints changed, and all together are as a bride prepared for her husband; and the nuptials are now solemnized.

All the promises and prophecies relating to the glorious state of the church are now fulfilled. The mystery of God, spoken by his servants, is finished. The kingdom of Christ is complete and

---

[1] From John Gill, *Exposition of the Old & New Testaments* (1809, Paris, AR: The Baptist Standard Bearer, 1989), 9:857–858 (commentary on Revelation 21:6).

[2] See Psalms 33:9.

all other kingdoms are destroyed. The day of redemption is come; the salvation of the saints is perfect. What was finished on the cross, by way of petition,[3] is now done as to application. All are saved with an everlasting salvation.

"I am Alpha and Omega, the beginning and the end"
(Revelation 21:6)

These words[4] are expressive of the primacy, perfection, and eternity of Christ; of his being the sum and substance, the first cause and last end of all things, relating both to the old and new world, to things temporal and spiritual.

"I will give unto him that is athirst of the fountain of the water of life freely" (Revelation 21:6)

He that is athirst is one that is so not in a natural—much less in a sinful—but in a spiritual sense. Such a person[5] has thirsted after Christ and salvation by him, after pardon of sin and a justifying righteousness, after communion with Christ and conformity to him and a greater

---

[3] Original: of impetration.
[4] Original: Which are.
[5] Original: Who as he has.

degree of knowledge of him. Likewise a person has thirsted[6] after the glories of his kingdom and the happiness of a future state.

To such a one Christ promises to give such large measures of grace and glory, and in such abundance, as will continue to refresh and delight and as may be compared to a fountain of living water; namely, for refreshment, abundance, and continuance. And all this he will give "freely," without money, and without price.[7] For as pardon and righteousness and the whole of salvation are all of free grace, so are all the enjoyments of the kingdom state: the riches, honours, and glories of it, and eternal life itself.

---

[6] Original: So after.
[7] See Isaiah 55:1.

26
What is prayer?[1]

Prayer is the breath of a regenerate soul; as soon as a child is born into the world it cries, as soon as a soul is born again it prays. It is observed of Saul upon his conversion, "Behold, he prayeth!"[2] Where there is life there is breath; where there is spiritual life there are spiritual breathings. Such souls breathe after God, pant after him as the deer[3] panteth after the water brooks.[4]

Prayer is the speech of the soul to God; a talking to him, a converse with him, in which much of its communion with God lies. Prayer is an address to God in the name of Christ, and through him as the Mediator under the influence and by the assistance of the Spirit of God, in faith, and in the sincerity of our souls. [Prayer asks] for such things we stand in need of and which are consistent with the will of God, and

---

[1] From John Gill, *A Body of Doctrinal and Practical Divinity* 5.5 (London: Thomas Tegg, 1839), 2:682.
[2] Acts 9:11.
[3] Original: hart
[4] See Psalm 42:1.

are for his glory to bestow, and therefore to be asked with submission.

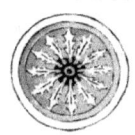

27
Some instructions on prayer[1]

It is proper to begin prayer[2] with a celebration and adoration of one or more of the divine perfections; which will at once have a tendency to strike our minds with a proper sense of the divine Majesty [to] glorify him, and [to] encourage us in our supplications to him; all which is highly necessary in our entrance on it. All the perfections of God are instructive to us in this work and serve to influence our minds and affections towards him, command our fear and reverence of him, engage our faith in him, strengthen our dependence on him, and raise in us expectations of receiving good things from him.

The greatness, glory, power, and majesty of God, the holiness, purity, and righteousness of

---

[1] From John Gill, *Two Discourses; the One On Prayer, the other On Singing of Psalms* (London: G. Keith & J. Robinson, 1751), 13–17.

[2] Original: this work

his nature, oblige us to a humble submission to him, and reverential awe of him. The consideration of his love, grace, mercy, and goodness, will not suffer his dread to make us afraid. We learn from his omniscience, that he knows not only our persons, but our wants, and what is most suitable for us, when the most convenient season, and which the best way and manner to bestow it on us.

It can be no small satisfaction to us that all things are naked and open unto the eyes of him with whom we have to do. The thoughts of our hearts are not hid from him, the secret effusions[3] of our minds are known to him, the breathings and desires of our souls are before him. He understands the language of a sigh and groan, and when we chatter like a crane or a swallow, it does not pass unobserved by him.

His omnipotence assures us that nothing is too hard for him, or impossible to him, [and] that he is able to do exceeding abundantly above all that we ask or think. [And] that we cannot be in such a low estate or distressed condition—or attended with such straits and difficulties—but he is able to relieve, deliver, and save us.

---

[3] Original: ejaculations

We conclude from his omnipresence that he fills the heavens and the earth, that he is in all places at all times, that he is a God at hand and a God afar off, that he is near unto us wherever we are, ready to assist us, and will be a very present help in trouble. His immutability in his counsel, and faithfulness in his covenant, yield the heirs of promise: strong consolation. These give us reason to believe that not one of the good things which the Lord has promised shall ever fail; that what he has said, he will do: and what he has either purposed or promised, he will bring to pass. He will not suffer his faithfulness to fail. His covenant he will not break, nor alter the thing that is gone out of his lips. …

In the next place, it highly becomes us to acknowledge our meanness and unworthiness, to make confession of our sins and transgressions, and pray for the fresh discoveries and manifestations of pardoning love and grace. When we enter into the divine presence, and take upon us to speak unto the Lord, we should own with Abraham that we are but dust and ashes;[4] and with Jacob that we are not worthy of the least of all the mercies and of all the truth

---

[4] See Genesis 18:27.

which God has showed unto us.[5] Confession of sin, both of our nature and of our lives, is a very proper and necessary part of this work. This has been the practice of the saints in all ages; as of David, which appears from his own words: "I acknowledge my sin unto thee, and mine iniquities have I not hid: I said, I will confess my transgressions unto the Lord, and thou forgavest the iniquity of my sin."[6] ...

Not that confession of sin is either the procuring cause, or means, or condition of pardon and cleansing, which are both owing to the blood of Christ; in justice and faithfulness to which, and him that shed it, God forgives the sins of his people, and cleanses them from them; but the design of the apostle is to show that sin is in the saints, and is committed by them, and that confession of sin is right and acceptable in the sight of God; and, to animate and encourage them to it, he takes notice of the justice and faithfulness of God in pardoning and cleansing his people, through the blood of Christ, which, as he had a little before observed, cleanseth from all sin.

---

[5] See Genesis 32:10.
[6] Psalm 32:5.

28
Further directions on prayer[1]

In a word, when we pray with our spirits, or in a spiritual way, we not only lift up our hearts to God—and what we ask for [we] ask in faith with a reverential, filial fear of the divine Majesty, in deep humility of soul, and with an entire submission to God's will—but also in the name and for the sake of our Lord Jesus Christ. We do not present our supplications to God for our righteousness' [sake], but for the Lord's sake, and for his great mercies.

We come not in our own name, but in Christ's. We go forth not in our own strength, but in his. We make mention of his righteousness and of his only. We plead the merits and efficacy of his blood; we bring his sacrifice in the arms of our faith; we expect audience and acceptance upon his account alone, and that our

---

[1] From John Gill, *Two Discourses; the One On Prayer, the other On Singing of Psalms* (London: G. Keith & J. Robinson, 1751), 27–28.

petitions and requests will be heard and answered for his sake and we leave them with him, who is our Advocate with the Father.

This may be called true, spiritual, fervent, and effectual prayer. Prayer cannot he performed in such a manner, without the grace, influence, and assistance of the Spirit of God. … [The Spirit] directs in the matter of prayer; for we know not what we should pray for as we ought; he maketh intercession for the saints according to the will of God.[2] And, indeed, who so proper as he, who searches the deep things of God, and perfectly knows his mind? He helps the saints under all their infirmities. When they are shut up in their souls and cannot come forth in prayer with liberty, he enlarges their hearts and gives them freedom of soul, and liberty of speech, so as they can pour out their souls before God and tell him all their mind. Where the Spirit of the Lord is, there is liberty.[3]

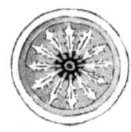

---

[2] See Romans 8:26–27.
[3] 2 Corinthians 3:17.

29
Encouragements to prayer[1]

God the Father, as the God of all grace, sits on the throne of grace, holding forth the sceptre of grace; inviting men to come thither where they may find grace and mercy to help them in their time of need.[2] Christ is the Mediator, through whom they have access to God, audience of him, and acceptance with him. Christ is their Advocate with the Father, who pleads their cause, and makes intercession for them. He introduces them into the presence of God, and as the Angel of his presence presents their prayers to God, perfumed with his much incense. And the Spirit of God is the Spirit of grace and of supplication who supplies them with grace and assists them in their supplications to God; and by whom—through Christ—they have access to God as their Father.

---

[1] From John Gill, *A Body of Doctrinal and Practical Divinity* 5.5 (London: Thomas Tegg, 1839), 2:693.
[2] See Hebrews 4:16.

From the interest saints have in God—to whom they pray—they have encouragement to it [in these ways]: he is their Father by adopting grace, whose heart is full of love, pity, and compassion; his heart is towards them, his eyes are upon them, and his ears are open to their cries; he is their covenant God and Father who has provided blessings in covenant for them, and is ready to distribute them upon their application to him by prayer.[3] ...

It is "good for saints to draw nigh to God."[4] It is not only good because it is their duty, but it is a pleasant good, when they have the presence of God in it and their souls are drawn out towards him. And it is a profitable good to them when God owns it as an ordinance, for the quickening the graces of his Spirit, subduing the corruptions of their hearts, and bringing them into nearer communion and fellowship with himself. Praying souls are profitable in families, in churches, in neighbourhoods, and commonwealths; whereas prayerless ones are useless, and obtain nothing, neither for themselves nor others. Of all the fruits which faith produces in

---

[3] See Philippians 4:19.
[4] Seems to be an amalgamation of Psalm 73:28 and James 4:8.

Christians, says Beza,[5] prayer—that is, calling on the name of God through Christ—is the principal one.

---

[5] Gill cites Theodore Beza, *Confession of Faith* 4.16.

A SERMON
IN
COMMEMORATION
OF THE
GREAT STORM,
In the Year MDCCIII.

Preach'd

In *Little Wild-street*, near *Lincoln's-Inn Fields*, Nov. 27, 1736.

By JOHN GILL.

LONDON:

Printed for AARON WARD, at the *King's-Arms*, in *Little-Britain*, MDCCXXXVII.
(Price Six-pence.)

30
Christ the Saviour from the tempest[1]

The occasion of this discourse is the great storm—commonly called the high wind—which arose the twenty-sixth and continued to the twenty-seventh of November, 1703, thirty three years ago. On the account of which, a day of humiliation was appointed by public authority, January the nineteenth following.

It is not easy to say what disasters and calamities it brought here and in other parts of Europe; how many edifices of a larger and lesser size were thrown down in cities, towns and villages; what devastations were made in parks, gardens and inclosures; how much shipping of greater and smaller bulk were destroyed; and,

---

[1] From John Gill, *A Sermon, In commemoration of the Great Storm, in the Year 1703: Preached in Little Wild-Street, near Lincoln's-Inn Fields, Nov. 27, 1736* in his *A Collection of Sermons and Tracts* (London: George Keith, 1773), 1:198–200.

what is of all most awful, what multitudes of souls, at once, launched into an endless eternity. ...

It is remarkable that on this very day, seven years ago, a considerable storm of wind arose which blew much about the same time this did, in its greatest fury, we now commemorate. I have reason to believe that there is one[2] here present who was cast away in it and remarkably delivered after having been exposed to the most imminent danger. I doubt not but such a one retains a sense of the mercy, and thankfully acknowledges the goodness of God, and the kind interposure of divine providence, in his favour. I shall close all with a word of exhortation.

Let us adore the perfections and observe the operations of Father, Son, and Spirit, in the government and management of the winds and seas. The concern that the Father of Christ has herein is not contested; nor need there be any

---

[2] Original footnote: "Mr. Robert Inger, a member of the church of Christ, at Horslydown, under my care, who was cast away on the Goodwin Sands, November 27, 1729, in the Endeavour, homeward bound from Virginia; who, with the whole ship's crew, in all seventeen, together with one passenger, and a pilot, were saved in a small pinnace [vessel], after they had been some hours exposed to the wind and sea, being taken up by a Deal vessel."

hesitation about the Son, when the instance, now attended to, is carefully considered. Nor should there be any [hesitation] about the Holy Ghost, when it is observed that the heavens were at first garnished by him, and he moved upon the face of the waters, and brought the present earth into the form and order in which it has since appeared. Besides, his extraordinary gifts bestowed upon the apostles on the day of Pentecost came down upon them with a rushing, mighty wind.[3] And the common—or ordinary—operations of his grace in the souls of men are compared to the wind: "The wind bloweth where it listeth, and thou hearest the sound thereof, but canst not tell whence it cometh and whither it goeth; so is every one that is born of the Spirit."[4] ...

Again, in the view of the awful dispensations of providence, let us humble ourselves before God, since these show the mighty hand of the Lord. Let us stand in awe of his righteous judgments. How soon—and how easy—can he make this large and populous city, and the whole

---

[3] See Acts 2:1.
[4] John 3:8.

kingdom, a heap of rubbish? Sanctify the Lord of hosts, make him your fear, and your dread.

To conclude, in a view of all our sins and transgressions, and of all that wrath and ruin they expose us to, let us take sanctuary in Christ. He is a strength to the poor, a strength to the needy in his distress, a refuge from the storm, a shadow from the heat.[5]

---

[5] See Isaiah 25:4.

31
On faith, hope, and love[1]

"And now abideth faith, hope, charity, these three"
(1 Corinthians 13:13)

These are the principal graces of the Spirit of God. Faith is to be understood, not as a faith of miracles—for that does not abide—nor of an historical one or mere assent to truth. Persons may have this faith and believe but for a while. But of that faith which is peculiar to God's elect; [it] is a fruit and effect of electing grace, and for that reason abides. [It] is the gift of God, and one of those which are without repentance. [It] is the work of God, and the operation of his Spirit, and therefore will be performed with power. It is the grace by which a soul sees Christ, goes unto him, lays hold on him, receives him, relies on him, and lives upon him.

"Hope" is also a gift of God's grace, implanted in regeneration. [It] has God and

---

[1] From John Gill, *Exposition of the Old & New Testaments* (1809, Paris, AR: The Baptist Standard Bearer, 1989), 8:710 (commentary on 1 Corinthians 13:13).

Christ—and not any worldly thing or outward performance—for its object, ground, and foundation, to build upon. It is of things unseen, future, difficult, yet possible to be enjoyed. It is supported by the love of God, is encouraged by promises, and is sure, being fixed on Christ and his righteousness. It is that grace by which saints wait for things promised and rejoice in the believing views of glory and happiness.

Charity designs love to God, Christ, and the saints. ... These are the three chief and leading graces in God's people, and they abide and continue with them. They may fail sometimes, as to their lively exercise, but never as to their being and principle. Faith may droop and hang its wing, hope may not be lively, and love may wax cold, but none[2] of them can be lost.

Christ prays that faith fail not. Hope on him is an anchor sure and steadfast, and nothing can separate from the love of Christ. As not from the love of Christ to his people, so not from theirs to him: these graces abide now during the present life. He that has true faith in Christ shall die in it, and he that has a good hope through grace shall have it in his death, and love will outlive

---

[2] Original: neither.

death and be in its height and glory in the other world. …

> *"But the greatest of these is charity"*
> *(1 Corinthians 13:13)*

Without charity,[3] faith and hope are nothing. And besides, its usefulness is more extensive than either of the other two. A man's faith is only for himself; a just man lives by his own faith, and not another's. One man's faith will be of no service to another, and the same is true of hope. But by love saints serve one another, both in things temporal and spiritual. And chiefly it is said to be the greatest because [it is the] most durable. In the other world, faith will be changed for vision, and hope for enjoyment, but love will abide and be in its full perfection and constant exercise, to all eternity.

---

[3] Original: this.

AN

EXPOSITION

OF THE

New Testament,

IN THREE VOLUMES:

IN WHICH

The Sense of the SACRED TEXT is given;

Doctrinal and Practical TRUTHS are set in a plain and easy Light,

DIFFICULT PLACES EXPLAINED,

SEEMING CONTRADICTIONS RECONCILED;

AND

Whatever is Material in the VARIOUS READINGS, and the several ORIENTAL VERSIONS, is observed.

THE

Whole illustrated with NOTES taken from the most ancient JEWISH WRITINGS.

VOL. I.

By *JOHN GILL.*

LONDON:
Printed for the AUTHOR,
And Sold by AARON WARD, at the *King's-Arms* in *Little-Britain.*

M.DCC.XLVI.

32
Christ is life[1]

"Jesus said unto her, I am the resurrection and the life" (John 11:25)

By these words, Jesus meant[2] that he was able of himself to raise men from death to life without asking it of his Father, and that he could do it now as well as at the general resurrection. ... This is true of Christ with regard to a spiritual resurrection, from a death of sin to a life of grace; he is concerned both in the life itself, and in the resurrection to it: he is the meritorious and procuring cause of it. He died for his people, that they—being dead to sin—might live unto God and unto righteousness. He is the author of it; he says unto them, when dead in sin, "live." He speaks life into them. He commands it in them, and by his Spirit breathes into them the breath of spiritual life ... and he supports and

---

[1] From John Gill, *Exposition of the Old & New Testaments* (1809, Paris, AR: The Baptist Standard Bearer, 1989), 8:25–26 (commentary on John 11:25).

[2] Original: Signifying that.

maintains it by giving himself to them as the bread of life to feed upon and by supplying them with grace continually. Yea, he himself is their life; he lives in them, and their life is hid with him.

"He that believeth in me, though he were dead, yet shall he live" (John 11:25)

Believers in Christ die as well as others, though death is not a penal evil to them. Its curse is removed, its sting is taken away—being satisfied for by Christ—and so becomes a blessing and privilege to them, and is desirable by them. But though they die, they shall live again. Their dust is under the peculiar care of Christ.

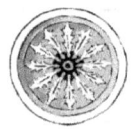

33
A principle of grace in the heart[1]

"Because in him there is found some good thing towards the Lord God of Israel" (1 Kings 14:13)

The Spirit of God is in his people as the author of the good work of grace upon their souls. In consequence of his being there, a new heart is given them; a new spirit is put within them, in which are new principles of grace, holiness, life, love, joy, peace, and comfort. New desires, new affections, new resolutions; all things are become new. This is the new creature, the new man the Scripture speaks of, which is no other than an assemblage of the several graces of the blessed Spirit. The fruits and graces of the Spirit are many. The principal of which are these three: faith, hope, and charity, or Love; but the greatest of them is love. Where one is, there are the others. Where faith—the principal, cardinal, leading grace—is, there is hope; for faith is the

---

[1] From John Gill, *A Principle of Grace in the Heart* in his *Sermons and Tracts* (London: W. Hardcastle, 1814), 2:215–227.

substance of things hoped for.[2] And there also is love; for faith works by love.[3] There are besides these several other graces, which, altogether, make up this good thing that is found in every regenerate man and which is towards the Lord God of Israel. ...

In some this good thing is very little, as at first conversion. It is a day of small things with newly regenerate persons: little knowledge, faith, hope, and the like; and therefore compared to the bruised reed and smoking flax. And yet, by these appearances, it is clear there is some good thing. In the bruised reed there is a moistness which shows it to be alive; in the smoking flax there are fire and heat. So in the lowest believer, in the exercise of grace in the weakest manner, there appears some good thing in him (though it is but little) towards the Lord God of Israel. Some light in him, though it is but small. A little knowledge of himself and the corruptions of his nature. A little knowledge of the person, offices, and excellencies of Christ. A little light in the doctrines of the everlasting gospel. ...

---

[2] See Hebrews 11:1.
[3] See Galatians 5:6.

The Lord knows the good thing he hath put into the hearts of his people, and he finds it. He sees not as man sees: he knows the heart, and sees what is in the heart. As it is said of our Lord, he knows what is in man.[4] He knew what good was in the heart of Peter; he knew how he loved him. Though there was but very little seen of it when he had so recently[5] and so basely denied him, yet he knew himself—he had love in his heart to Christ—and he knew that Christ was acquainted with it. "Lord" (says he), "thou knowest all things, thou knowest that I love thee."[6] So wherever there is any good—ever so small—towards the God of Israel, God will find it out because he put it there. …

And I am persuaded, that there is in many persons some good thing towards the Lord God of Israel that does not appear now, and—it may be—may never appear to satisfaction in this world. And yet [it] will be found at the great day of accounts, when God will bring to light the hidden things of darkness and make manifest the secrets of every heart; what he had wrought there.

---

[4] See John 2:25.
[5] Original: so lately.
[6] See John 21:15–17.

34
Dying thoughts[1]

The life of a common believer is a well-spent life in comparison to others. He lives by faith on Christ and gives him the glory of his salvation and—from a principle of love to him—walks in all his commandments and ordinances. He is very desirous of living a life of holiness and of spiritual and heavenly-mindedness, and does so live in some measure. But when the believer comes to look back on his past life of faith and holiness, what deficiencies and imperfections in his faith! What unbelief in him, at such and such a time will he observe! What tarnishes in his life and walk! And how few the minutes were in which he was spiritual and heavenly-minded! And how frequently and long was such a frame interrupted with carnal and sensual lusts?

---

[1] From John Gill, *Dying Thoughts* in his *A Collection of Sermons and Tracts* (London: George Keith, 1773), 2:585–591.

The saint before his conversion is as other men; being born in sin and living in it. After conversion, [he is] prone to backsliding. Even in all things he offends; and sins in his most solemn and religious services. He must therefore betray great ignorance of himself who flatters himself or suffers himself to be flattered with a reflection on a well-spent life. ...

Death is very terrible to nature, and to natural men. The philosopher calls it the most terrible of all terribles. And the wise man, when he suggests what is most grievous, distressing, and intolerable, says, "What is more bitter than death?"[2] To Christless sinners, death is the king of terrors. And even some gracious persons are all their lifetime, through fear of death, subject to bondage. But as formidable as it is, there are some things which may serve to fortify us against the fears of death:

1. That the sting of death is taken away by Christ. The sting[3] is sin; and a very venomous sting it is. And death, thus armed, is to be feared. But when its sting is taken out, it is not to be dreaded. Any insect with a sting we are naturally

---

[2] Ecclesiastes 7:26.
[3] Original: Which is.

afraid of, but if its sting is drawn, we have no fear of it though it flies and buzzes about us. The believer will sing and say, "Death where is thy sting?" and be fearless of it.

2. It is a blessing and privilege to a believer, it is reckoned among his privileges,[4] they are blessed that die in the Lord; and are more happy than the saints alive, because [they are] free from sin and sorrow.[5]

3. Death is but once, and soon over. The bitterness of it is quickly past and will never be repeated. It is appointed to men once to die, and no more.[6]

4. The consideration of the resurrection from the dead may yield comfort in the view of death, as it did to Job.[7] The body—though a vile body as laid in the grave—will be raised and fashioned like to the glorious body of Christ. It will be raised in incorruption: this corruptible shall put on incorruption. It will be raised in glory, like Christ. It will be raised in power and be durable, and always remain in a state of immortality. It will be raised a spiritual body, and

---

[4] See 1 Corinthians 3:22.
[5] See Revelation 14:13. Ecclesiastes 4:2.
[6] See Hebrews 9:27.
[7] See Job 19:26–27.

so more fit for spiritual services than ever,⁸ so that the saints will be no losers, but gainers by death; and need not fear it.

5. Be it that death is an enemy, as it is contrary to nature, it is the last enemy that shall be destroyed. And when that is conquered the victory will be complete over every enemy, sin, Satan, the world, death and the grave.⁹ Thanks, therefore, to God, who giveth us the victory through our Lord Jesus Christ.

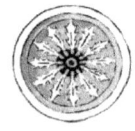

---

⁸ See 1 Corinthians 15:42–43.
⁹ 1 Corinthians 15:26, 55, 57.

35
Last words[1]

As he lay on his deathbed, John Gill wrote the following in a letter to his nephew:

> I depend wholly and alone upon the free, sovereign, eternal, unchangeable, love of God, the firm and everlasting covenant of grace, and my interest in the Persons of the sacred Trinity, for my whole salvation; and not upon any righteousness of my own; nor anything in me, or done by me under the influences of the Holy Spirit; not upon any services of mine, which I have been assisted to perform for the good of the church, but upon my interest in the Persons of the Trinity; the free grace of God, and the blessings of grace streaming to me through the blood and righteousness of Christ, as the ground of my hope. These

---

[1] From John Rippon, *A Brief Memoir of the Life and Writings of the Late Rev. John Gill, D. D.* (London: Bennett, 1838), 132–133.

are no new things to me, but what I have been long acquainted with; what I can live and die by. I apprehend I shall not be long here, but this you may tell to any of my friends.

Nearly in the same words he expressed himself to other friends. To one, he said, "I have nothing to make me uneasy." And then repeated the following lines from Dr. Watts, in honour of the adored Redeemer.

> He rais'd me from the depths of sin,—
>   The gates of gaping hell;
> And fix'd my standing more secure
>   Than 'twas before I fell.[2]

This tranquility of soul, this internal joy and peace of mind, never left him. The last words he was heard to speak were: "O my Father, my Father!"

---

[2] Isaac Watts, "Arise, my soul, my joyful powers." This hymn first appeared in Isaac Watts, *Hymns and Spiritual Songs* (London, 1707), Book 2, no. 82, in 6 stanzas of 4 lines. It was originally titled "Redemption and Protection from Spiritual Enemies."

Appendix 1

An Account of some Choice Experiences of Elizabeth Gill, who departed this Life May 30, 1738, having entered the Thirteenth Year of her Age

Elizabeth Gill, daughter of John and Elizabeth Gill, was born March 14, 1725–1726. She appeared from her infancy to be a child of a sweet disposition, of great solidity and thoughtfulness, of a quick understanding, and retentive memory. She was much reserved and greatly delighted in retirement and solitude, was not addicted to play as children usually are, and if at any time she amused herself with the innocent diversions of her age, it was not in company with the rude and vain but with the more sober and civilized sort of children.

As she grew up, she took much delight in reading good books such as Bunyan's *Pilgrim's Progress*, Janeway's *A Token for Children*,[1] and

---

[1] The full title gives the reader a sense for the content of the book: *A Token for Children, Being An Exact Account of the Conversion, Holy and Exemplary Lives and Joyful Deaths, of Several Young Children.*

others of the like kind. She observed the difference there was between some children and others; how, that some as soon as they began to speak, and before they could speak plain, learned bad words, and took the name of God in vain; while others were religiously inclined, and thoughtful about a future state; of which number she earnestly desired to be. She took great notice in hearing the Word, and would afterwards repeat many things to her mother. She was a diligent observer of what passed in Christian conversation; and among other things remarked, that the conversion of the people of God was sometimes occasioned by dreams, which made them reflect carefully[2] about the welfare of their immortal souls. This made her greatly desire that the like might be the means of her conversion.

Accordingly, sometime later[3] she dreamed, and in her dream had a view both of heaven and hell. The smoke of the latter came out in a most dreadful manner, and greatly terrified her. She spied, as she thought, her schoolmistress—a gracious good woman—in heaven, having some

---

[2] Original: which put them on close thinking.

[3] Original: sometime after.

reviving drops in her bosom. Thither she wanted to get, and at length did get to her, where she thought herself in a most glorious place and happy condition. Sometime later[4] she dreamed again that a man on horseback appeared to her in a most terrible manner, threatening to kill her; at which she was not at all daunted but quietly and cheerfully submitted to the stroke of death. Suddenly she found herself in a most delightful place, where were an abundance of people walking to and fro. But she observed that they took no notice of one another nor said anything to each other. When she awoke, she wished herself again in that pleasant place.

This was about two years ago. Though she had had many thoughts before about a future state, after this she began to think more closely of it. This put her upon seeking and praying to God, that he would, as she expressed herself, give her grace; of which she was encouraged by those words, "Ask, and it shall be given you; seek, and ye shall find; knock, and it shall be opened to you."[5]

---

[4] Original: Sometime after.
[5] Matthew 7:7.

It pleased God now to show her [the] vileness, sinfulness, and unworthiness, and the wickedness of her heart and nature. For notwithstanding all her solidity and sobriety, which seemed to be as it were natural to her, she thought herself one of the wickedest creatures upon earth. When she heard that her aforementioned schoolmistress should say of her, "Surely that child was sanctified from the womb;" she thought within herself; "Am I, Oh! She does not know how bad I am; what a wicked heart I have."

What follows is a remarkable instance of her sense of sin and the tenderness of her conscience, as well as God's sealing his pardoning grace to her soul.[6] It happened that,[7] her brother standing in her way, she bid him remove. Instead of doing which, he smiled at her, and gave her no answer. Upon that she said to him, "The boy stands like a fool." But O! What effect did that word "fool" have[8] in her poor conscience. She had no rest night or day for some time after, until it pleased God to apply to her, while she was crying alone by herself, those words: "I will

---

[6] Original: A remarkable instance… to her soul, is what follows.

[7] Original: At a certain time.

[8] Original: work did that word fool make.

pardon thine iniquity, and will remember thy sins no more,"[9] which calmed her conscience and quieted her mind.

Her desires for Christ, and an interest in him grew very strong. She found in her soul a very great affection for him. She would sometimes say within herself; "I love him. Methinks I could hug him in my arms." She thought it was a hard thing to come to Christ. But she sometimes hoped she had an interest in him, though she dared[10] not say she had, for fears attended her. But on her deathbed, discoursing with her father about divine things, she dropped those appropriating words, "Christ died for me," which being observed by him, he said to her, "My dear, can you say, Christ died for you?" "Yes," said she, "Christ died for me." Nay, one time she said, she thought she even saw Christ when those words were made of wonderful use to her, "For yet a little while, and he that shall come, will come, and will not tarry."[11]

She had many sweet words of Scripture brought home to her soul which yielded her much spiritual refreshment. Among the rest,

---

[9] Jeremiah 31:34.
[10] Original: she durst not.
[11] Hebrews 10:37.

that portion of Scripture, "I will strengthen thee; yea, I will help thee; yea, I will uphold thee with the right hand of my righteousness,"[12] was made very useful to her in a time of great distress. For being in great indisposition of body, and knowing what was coming upon her, and what she must go through, [she] was much discouraged. But those words being set home upon her heart, she was much encouraged, cheerfully went through what she so much feared, and felt but little pain.

Sometimes she would be afraid that the passages of Scriptures which came to her mind did not come in the right way—from the Spirit of God—but were what she had heard or read, and so thought of them again. She would listen with great attention and pleasure to the people of God, when discoursing about their experience of the grace of God, and would oftentimes observe to herself that her case and theirs was alike, and that she felt and experienced the same things as they did, which gave her great satisfaction.

She had a great desire for—and a wonderful esteem of—the grace of humility, both in things temporal and spiritual. She admired it in others

---

[12] Isaiah 41:10.

and wished for it in herself. She desired not to have a proud look, or conduct,[13] or to behave herself proudly in any respect. She thought within herself that should she live to be a woman, and God should bless her with anything of this world, she should choose to go neat and clean, but would not spend her money in fine clothes. But what she could spare would give to good people that were poor.

And as to things spiritual, she was always fearful, lest any pride or vanity should appear in her: hence she was shy of speaking of what God had done for her lest it should seem or be thought to arise from pride, and so be a matter of boasting. Hence she studiously affected to retire into corners, to read good books, and to desire of God to give her his grace. Frequently her bed, and time of sleep and rest, were the place and time of her serious and deepest meditations. For then, to use her own words, she could privately speak to herself. And God did clothe her with humility and gave her the ornament of a meek and quiet spirit, which is in his sight of great price.[14] And to the last she entertained a

---

[13] Original: carriage.
[14] See 1 Peter 3:4.

mean and low opinion of herself. When it was told her that such and such had prayed for her, and such and such[15] had prayed for her, she would say, "What, think of me! What, pray for me! Such an unworthy creature as I am!"

She expressed a very great veneration and respect for the hearing of the Word and other ordinances of the gospel. When at any time while[16] hearing the Word she found her heart wandering and her thoughts diverted to other things, as she sometimes did—whereby she lost much of what was spoken—it was a grief and trouble to her. And since her illness, how she has longed to enjoy opportunities of hearing the gospel preached, which she hoped to do with more attention and profit. Her father repeating in the family one Lord's day evening the heads of a sermon he had preached that day on Proverbs 8:34: "Blessed is the man that heareth me, watching daily at my gates, waiting at the posts of my door"—it was made of much use to her.

Two things she particularly observed. The one was the necessity and usefulness of hearing the Word, in order to the knowledge of Christ,

---

[15] Original: such an one [twice in this sentence].
[16] Original: under.

and faith in him, which was proved from Romans 10:14, "How shall they believe in him, of whom they have not heard?" And the other was the encouragement given to poor souls to wait upon the ministry of the Word, taken from the instance of the poor man's waiting at the pool of Bethesda, who had an infirmity thirty-eight years, and at last had a cure.[17]

At a certain time she and her brother, having seen the ordinance of baptism administered by their father, talked together about it. Her brother said he would not care to be baptized for he would be afraid. But, thought she within herself, if things were but right with me—if I had but a true knowledge of things—I would not be afraid; I would gladly be baptized. And sometimes she would think what[18] a delightful thing it would be, should she go to the Lord's supper and partake of it with the saints and people of God. When she related this to her father on her deathbed, he being somewhat fearful, lest she should then labor under any discouragements, because she had not been baptized, nor had partook of the Lord's supper, told her that though

---

[17] A reference to John 5:1–9.
[18] Original: think with herself.

these are ordinances of Christ, and ought to be complied with, and submitted to by all that believe in Christ who are proper subjects of them, and are satisfied of their right to them, as they have health and opportunity, yet salvation does not depend upon them. Persons may be saved without them through the grace of Christ, who have not an opportunity of submitting to them, to which she assented and seemed very well satisfied.

She was greatly affected with the goodness, grace, and mercy of God in taking such notice of and giving his Son for such a sinful, unworthy creature as she thought herself to be. She expressed much thankfulness for temporal mercies and took great notice of the common mercies of life. When she rose in the morning she would think to[19] herself what a mercy it was that she had been refreshed with rest and preserved in the night season from fire and other dangers.

Her afflictions, pains, and agonies—which were many and great—were borne by her, in her illness, with much patience. Though she would sometimes complain she had not and was fearful she should not have patience enough.

---

[19] Original: with herself.

Sometimes she would think of the holy martyrs and of their sufferings: "O!" says she, "What did they suffer! How were they burnt for Christ? With what patience did they endure? O! that I had but patience to bear what God is pleased to lay upon me."

Death was no king of terrors to her. She did not seem to have the least fear of it nor in any respect or on any account to be intimidated by it. She often expressed her willingness to die and her readiness to submit to the will of God, and would observe that God sometimes makes persons willing to die before they do, which was her case. Nor could she see, she said, anything in this world that was desirable for which she might wish to live. And if at any time she expressed any desire to live,[20] she added it was only for her mother's sake, who she knew would be greatly troubled at her death. Yea, she longed to be gone and would often pour out her soul in private effusions[21] to her dear Lord with whom she desired to be. Her sister once observing her lips to move, as they often would when no voice was heard, said to her, "My dear, did you say

---

[20] Original: signified any desire of living.
[21] Original: ejaculations.

anything?" "No," says she, "I was not speaking to you, nor to anybody else. I was speaking to my dear Lord." In this frame she continued to the last, as long as she was conscious.[22] And on Tuesday, May 30th, [she] sweetly fell asleep in Jesus, aged twelve years, two months, and sixteen days.

The dream she had of the man on horseback was a lively emblem of her death and the manner of it. Death seems to be represented by him, at whose awful stroke she was not in the least dismayed, but quietly submitted to it. And no doubt [she] finds herself in that delightful place she thought herself to be in then, where God has given her "places to walk among [those] that stand by" (Zech. 3:7). These things, with many others which cannot be perfectly recollected, were related by her on her deathbed to her father and mother with whom only she had freedom of speech about spiritual things.

One thing is very remarkable, that while she was discoursing about these matters, as she sometimes would an hour or an hour and a half together, she was quite another person. Her spirits would revive, a briskness appeared in her

---

[22] Original: sensible.

countenance, she seemed to have no pain. Nor was the least groan or complaint heard from her all the while, nor any appearance of even weariness throughout the whole interval, and [she] would for some time after continue better and more cheerful though before her agonies were very great. And she would also observe that when she had pleasant thoughts, as she called them, she felt no pain.

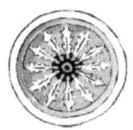

CARTER LANE CHAPEL

Appendix 2

Declaration of the Faith and Practice of the Church of Christ, in Carter-Lane, Southwark, under the Pastoral Care of Dr. John Gill, Read and assented to, at the Admission of Members

Having been enabled, through divine grace, to give up ourselves to the Lord, and likewise to one another by the will of God, we account it a duty incumbent upon us, to make a declaration of our faith and practice, to the honour of Christ, and the glory of his name; knowing, that as with the heart man believeth unto righteousness, so with the mouth confession is made unto salvation;[1] a which declaration is as follows, viz.,

---

[1] Romans 10:10.

I

We believe, that the Scriptures of the Old and New Testament, are[2] the Word of God, and the only[3] rule of faith and practice.

II

We believe, that there is but one[4] only living and true God: that there are[5] three persons in the Godhead, the Father, the Son, and the Holy Ghost, who are equal in nature, power, and glory; and that the Son[6] and the Holy Ghost[7] are as truly and properly God as the Father. These three divine persons are distinguished from each other, by peculiar relative properties: the distinguishing character and relative property of the first person is begetting; he has begotten a Son of the same nature with him, and who is the

---

[2] 2 Timothy 3:15–17; 2 Peter 1:21.

[3] John 5:39; Acts 17:11; 2 Peter 1:19, 20.

[4] Deuteronomy 6:4; 1 Corinthians 8:6; 1 Timothy 2:5; Jeremiah 10:10.

[5] 1 John 5:7; Matthew 28:19.

[6] John 10:30; Philippians 2:6; Romans 9:5; 1 John 5:20.

[7] Acts 5:3, 4; 1 Corinthians 3:16, 17; 2 Corinthians 3:17, 18.

express image of his person;[8] and therefore is with great propriety called the Father. The distinguishing character and relative property of the second person is that he is begotten; and he is called the only begotten of the Father, and his own proper Son;[9] not a Son by creation, as angels and men are, nor by adoption, as saints are, nor by office, as civil magistrates; but by nature, by the Father's eternal generation[10] of him in the divine nature; and therefore he is truly called the Son. The distinguishing character and relative property of the third person is to be breathed by the Father and the Son, and to proceed from both,[11] and is very Properly called the Spirit, or breath of both. These three distinct divine persons, we profess to reverence, serve, and worship as the one true God.[12]

---

[8] Psalm 2:7; Hebrews 1:3.

[9] John 1:14; Romans 8:3, 32.

[10] Psalm 2:7.

[11] Job 33:4; Psalm 33:6; John 15:26; 20:26; 20:22; Galatians 4:6.

[12] 1 John 5:7; Matthew 4:10.

III

We believe, that before the world began God did elect[13] a certain number of men unto everlasting salvation whom he did predestinate to the adoption of children by Jesus Christ of his own free grace, and according to the good pleasure of his will; and that in pursuance of this gracious design, he did contrive and make a covenant[14] of grace and peace with his son Jesus Christ, on the behalf of those persons; wherein a Saviour[15] was appointed, and all spiritual[16] blessings provided for them; as also that their[17] persons, with all their grace[18] and glory, were put into the hands of Christ, and made his care and charge.

---

[13] Ephesians 1:4; 1 Thessalonians 1:4 and 5:9; 2 Thessalonians 2:13; Romans 8:30; Ephesians 1:5; 1 John 3:1; Galatians 4:4, 5; John 1:12.

[14] 2 Samuel 23:5; Psalm 89:2, 28, 34; Isaiah 42:6.

[15] Psalm 89:19; Isaiah 49:6.

[16] 2 Samuel 23:5; Isaiah 55:3; Ephesians 1:3.

[17] Deuteronomy 33:3; John 6:37, 39 and 10:28, 29; Jude 1.

[18] 2 Timothy 1:9; Ephesians 1:3; Colossians 3:3, 4.

IV

We believe, that God created the first man, Adam, after his image, and in his likeness, an upright, holy, and innocent creature, capable of serving and glorifying him:[19] but he sinning, all his posterity sinned in him, and came short of the glory of God;[20] the guilt of whose sin is imputed;[21] and a corrupt nature derived to all his offspring descending from him by ordinary and natural generation;[22] that they are by their first birth carnal and unclean; averse to all that is good, incapable of doing any, and prone to every[23] sin; and are also by nature children of wrath, and under a sentence of condemnation;[24] and so are subject, not only to a corporal death,[25] and involved in a moral one, commonly called spiritual;[26] but are also liable to an eternal

---

[19] Genesis 1:26, 27; Ecclesiastes 7:29; Psalm 8:5.
[20] Romans 5:12; 3:23.
[21] Romans 5:12, 14, 18, 19; 1 Corinthians 15:22; Ephesians 2:3.
[22] Job 14:4; Psalm 51:5; John 3:6; Ezekiel 16:4-6.
[23] Romans 8:7, 8 and 3:10-12; Genesis 6:5.
[24] Ephesians 2:3; Romans 5:12, 18.
[25] Genesis 2:7; Romans 5:12, 14; Hebrews 9:27.
[26] Matthew 8:21; Luke 15:24, 32; John 5:25; Ephesians 3:1.

death,[27] as considered in the first Adam, fallen and sinners; from all which there is no deliverance, but by Christ, the second Adam.[28]

V

We believe, that the Lord Jesus Christ, being set up from[29] everlasting as the Mediator of the covenant, and he having engaged to be the[30] Surety of his people, did in the fullness of time, really assume[31] human nature, and not before, neither in whole, nor in part; his human soul being a creature, existed not from eternity, but was created and formed in his body by him that forms the spirit of man within him, when that was conceived in the womb of the virgin; and so his human nature consists of a true body and a reasonable soul; both which, together and at once the Son of God assumed into union with his divine person, when made of a woman, and not before;

---

[27] Romans 5:18 and 6:23; Ephesians 2:3.
[28] Romans 6:23 and 7:24, 25 and 8:2; 2 Timothy 1:10; 1 Corinthians 15:45, 47.
[29] Proverbs 8:22, 23; Hebrews 12:24.
[30] Psalm 49:6-8; Hebrews 7:22.
[31] Hebrews 2:14, 16, 17.

in which nature he really suffered, and died[32] as the substitute of his people, in their room and stead; whereby he made all that satisfaction[33] for their sins, which the law and justice of God could require; as well as made way for all those blessings[34] which are needful for them both for time and eternity.

VI

We believe, that eternal Redemption which Christ has obtained by the shedding of his blood[35] is special and particular; that is to say, that it was only intentionally designed for the elect of God, and sheep of Christ, who only share the special and peculiar blessings of it.

---

[32] Romans 4:25; 1 Corinthians 15:3; Ephesians 5:2; 1 Peter 3:18.
[33] Romans 8:3, 4 and 10:4; Isaiah 42:21; Romans 8:1, 33, 34.
[34] 1 Corinthians 1:30; Ephesians 1:7.
[35] Matthew 20:28; John 10:11, 15; Revelation 5:9; Romans 8:30.

VII

We believe, that the justification of God's elect, is only by the righteousness[36] of Christ imputed to them, without the consideration of any works of righteousness done by them; and that the full and free pardon of all their sins and transgressions, past, present, and to come, is only through the blood of Christ,[37] according to the riches of his grace.

VIII

We believe, that the work of regeneration, conversion, sanctification, and faith, is not an act of[38] man's free will and power, but of the mighty, efficacious, and irresistible grace[39] of God.

---

[36] Romans 3:28 and 4:6 and 5:16–19.
[37] Romans 3:25; Ephesians 1:7; Colossians 2:13; 1 John 1:7, 9.
[38] John 1:13; Romans 9:16 and 8:7.
[39] Philippians 2:13; 2 Timothy 1:9; James 1:18; 1 Peter 1:3; Ephesians 1:19; Isaiah 43:13.

IX

We believe, that all those, who are chosen by the Father, redeemed by the Son, and sanctified by the Spirit, shall certainly and finally[40] persevere; so that not one of them shall ever perish, but shall have everlasting life.

X

We believe, that there will be a resurrection of the dead;[41] both of the just and unjust; and that Christ will come a second time to judge[42] both quick and dead; when he will take vengeance on the wicked, and introduce his own people into his kingdom and glory, where they shall be forever with him.

---

[40] Matthew 24:24; John 6:39, 40 and 10:28, 29; Matthew 16:18; Psalm 125:1, 2; 1 Peter 1:5; Jude 24; Hebrews 2:13; Romans 8:30.

[41] Acts 24:15; John 5:28, 29; Daniel 12:2.

[42] Hebrews 9:28; Acts 17:31; 2 Timothy 4:1; 2 Thessalonians 1:7–10; 1 Thessalonians 4:15-17.

XI

We believe, that Baptism[43] and the Lord's Supper are ordinances of Christ, to be continued until his second coming; and that the former is absolutely requisite to the latter; that is to say, that those [44]only are to be admitted into the communion of the church, and to participate of all ordinances in it,[45] who upon profession of their faith, have been baptized,[46] by immersion, in the name of the Father,[47] and of the Son, and of the Holy Ghost.

XII

We also believe, that singing of psalms, hymns, and spiritual songs vocally[48] is an ordinance of the Gospel, to be performed by believers; but

---

[43] Matthew 28:19, 20; 1 Corinthians 11:23–26.

[44] Acts 2:41 and 9:18, 26.

[45] Mark 16:16; Acts 8:12, 36, 37; 16:31–34; 8:8.

[46] Matthew 3:6, 16; John 3:23; Acts 8:38, 39; Romans 6:4; Colossians 2:12.

[47] Matthew 28:19.

[48] Matthew 26:30; Acts 16:25; 1 Corinthians 14:15, 26; Ephesians 5:19; Colossians 3:16.

that as to time, place, and manner, every one ought to be left to their[49] liberty in using it.

* * *

Now all and each of these doctrines and ordinances, we look upon ourselves under the greatest obligation to embrace, maintain, and defend; believing it to be our duty[50] to stand fast in one spirit, with one mind, striving together for the faith of the Gospel.

And whereas we are very sensible, that our conversation, both in the world and in the church, ought to be as becometh the Gospel of Christ;[51] we judge it our incumbent duty, to[52] walk in wisdom towards them that are without, to exercise a conscience[53] void of offence towards God and men, by living[54] soberly, righteously, and godly in this present world.

---

[49] James 5:13.
[50] Philippians 1:27; Jude 3.
[51] Philippians 1:27.
[52] Colossians 4:5.
[53] Acts 24:16.
[54] Titus 2:12.

And as to our regards to each other, in our church-communion; we esteem it our duty to[55] walk with, each other in all humility and brotherly love; to watch[56] over each other's conversation; to stir up one[57] another to love and good works; not forsaking the assembling of ourselves together, as we have opportunity, to worship God according to his revealed will; and, when the case requires, to warn,[58] rebuke, and admonish one another, according to the rules of the Gospel.

Moreover, we think ourselves obliged[59] to sympathize with each other, in all conditions, both inward and outward, which God, in his providence, may bring us into; as also to[60] bear with one another's weaknesses, failings and infirmities; and particularly to pray for one another,[61] and that the Gospel, and the ordinances thereof, might be blessed to the edification and

---

[55] Ephesians 4:1–3; Romans 12:9, 10, 16; Philippians 2:2, 3.

[56] Leviticus 19:17; Philippians 2:4.

[57] Hebrews 10:24, 25.

[58] 1 Thessalonians 5:14; Romans 15:14; Leviticus 19:17; Matthew 18:15–17.

[59] Romans 12:15; 1 Corinthians 12:26.

[60] Romans 15:1; Ephesians 4:12; Colossians 3:13.

[61] Ephesians 6:18, 19; 2 Thessalonians 3:1.

comfort of each other's souls, and for the gathering in of others to Christ, besides those who are already gathered.

All which duties we desire to be found in the performance of, through the gracious assistance of the Holy Spirit whilst we both admire and adore the grace, which has given us a place, and a name in God's house, better than that of sons and daughters.[62]

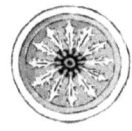

---

[62] Isaiah 56:5.

Reading spiritual classics

In recent days, "spirituality" has become something of a buzzword in society. People seem concerned about the deeper "soul" realities of life. This is encouraging to see but there is a downside as well. The spiritual books being read are quite often drawn from streams that are seriously deficient when it comes to the truths Reformed believers delight in. This series has been designed to partially fill this gap by providing choice selections from various Reformed writers.

The reading of spiritual classics should differ from other types of reading. One reads a newspaper, dictionary or textbook for factual information or immediate answers to questions but in spiritual reading one seeks to inflame the heart towards God as well as to inform the mind. Spiritual reading, as Eugene Peterson has noted, should therefore be "leisurely, repetitive, reflective reading"—it should not be hurried. Careful attention needs to be paid to what the Spirit of God is saying through the text and those readings which are rich in spiritual nourishment need to be re-read again and again.

Of course, when it comes to spiritual classics, the Bible occupies a unique and indispensable place—it is the fountainhead and source of the Christian faith. Anyone wishing to make progress as a disciple of Christ must be committed to regular reflection and meditation on the Scriptures. As David says in Psalm 1, a believer is truly blessed when he or she delights in the Word of God and meditates on it "day and night" (Psalm 1:1–2).

Christians, for many generations now, have found strength and nourishment by meditating on the Word of God. Often their wisdom and insight was recorded—either in books, diaries, letters, hymns or sermons—and some of these, having been preserved, we are in the habit of calling spiritual classics. Such classics have a way of sending their readers back to the Bible with deeper insight into the nature of the Christian faith and serve to cultivate a greater desire to seek after Christ's glory and his abiding presence in their lives.

—*Michael A.G. Haykin*

Select Bibliography

Brush, John W. "John Gill's Doctrine of the Church." In *Baptist Concepts of the Church*, ed. Winthrop S. Hudson, 53–70. Philadelphia, PA: Judson Press, 1959.

Daniel, Curt. "Hyper-Calvinism and John Gill." PhD dissertation, University of Edinburgh, 1983.

Ella, George M. *John Gill and the Cause of God and Truth*. Eggleston, England: Go Publications, 1995.

George, Timothy. "John Gill." In *Theologians of the Baptist Tradition*, ed. Timothy George and David S. Dockery, Rev. ed., 11–33. Nashville, TN: Broadman & Holman, 2001.

Gill, John. *A Body of Doctrinal and Practical Divinity*. 1810, Paris, AK: Baptist Standard Bearer, 2007.

___. *A Collection of Sermons and Tracts*. London: George Keith, 1773 & 1778. 3 vols.

___. *An Exposition of the Book of Solomon's Song*. 1854, Paris, AR: Baptist Standard Bearer, 2008.

___. *Exposition of the Old & New Testaments*. 9 vols. 1809–1810; Paris, AR: Baptist Standard Bearer, 1989.

Harrison, Graham. *Dr. John Gill and His Teaching*, Annual Lecture of The Evangelical Library. London: The Evangelical Library, 1971.

Haykin, Michael A. G., ed. *The Life and Thought of John Gill (1697–1771): A Tercentennial Appreciation*. Leiden: Brill, 1997.

Helm, Paul. "The Gift of Gill" [online]. Accessed May 16, 2022. Available from http://paulhelmsdeep.blogspot.com/2008/12/analysis-22-gift-of-gill-john-gill-1697.html; Internet.

Mickle, Allen. "'A Fountain of Gardens, a Well of Living Waters': A Survey of Christian Spirituality from John Gill's Exposition of the Book of Solomon's Song." Paper presented at the annual conference of the Andrew Fuller Center, Louisville, Kentucky, August 24–25, 2009.

Nettles, Thomas J. *By His Grace and For His Glory: A Historical, Theological, and Practical Study of the Doctrines of Grace in Baptist Life*. Cape Coral, Florida: Founders Press, 2006.

Oliver, Robert. "John Gill: Orthodox Dissenter." *The Strict Baptist Historical Society Bulletin* 23 (1996): 3–18.

Park, Hong-Gyu. "Grace and Nature in the Theology of John Gill (1697–1771)." PhD dissertation, University of Aberdeen, 2001.

Rathel, David Mark. "John Gill and the Charge of Hyper-Calvinism: Assessing Contemporary Arguments in Defense of Gill in Light of Gill's Doctrine of Eternal Justification." *The Southern Baptist Journal of Theology* 25, no.1 (Spring 2021): 43–62.

Rippon, John. *Life and Writings of the Rev. John Gill, D.D.* 1838, Harrisonburg, VA: Sprinkle Publications, 2006.

Robison, Olin C. "The Legacy of John Gill." *Baptist Quarterly* 24, no. 3 (July 1971): 111–125.

Seymour, Robert E. "John Gill, Baptist Theologian." PhD dissertation, University of Edinburgh, 1954.

White, B.R. "John Gill in London, 1719–1729: A Biographical Fragment." *The Baptist Quarterly* 22 (1967–68): 72–91.

Scripture Index

Old Testament

Genesis
- 1:26 175
- 1:27 175
- 2:7 175
- 6:5 175
- 18:27 129
- 32:10 130

Leviticus
- 19:17 182

Deuteronomy
- 6:4 172
- 6:5 .... 81, 82
- 33:3 174

1 Samuel
- 18:1 58

2 Samuel
- 23:5 174

1 Kings
- 14:13 147

2 Chronicles
- 15:2 120

Job
- 14:4 175
- 19:26–27 41
- 19:26–27 153
- 33:4 ...... 100, 173

Psalms
- 2:7 .... 99, 173
- 8:5 175
- 17:15 56
- 18:1 117
- 22:1 65
- 22:13–14 77
- 22:8 67
- 31:3 117
- 32:1 48
- 32:5 130
- 33:6 ...... 100, 173
- 33:9 121
- 42:1 125
- 49:6-8 176
- 51:1 .... 43, 44
- 51:5 175
- 73:25 96
- 73:28 134
- 89:2 174
- 89:19 174
- 89:28 174
- 89:34 174
- 97:12 85

103:1 .... 83, 84
103:1–2 83
125:1 179
125:2 179
130:1 75

Proverbs
8:22 176
8:23 176
8:34— 164
25:11 115

Ecclesiastes
4:2 153
7:26 152
7:29 175

Song of Solomon
1:4 28
1:8 70
2:1 .... 69, 73
2:3 118
2:16 117
4:2 29
4:10 70
5:4-5 116
8:6 82

Isaiah
3:10 48
25:4 140
35:1 70
41:10 162
42:6 174
42:21 177

43:13 178
45:24 .... 50, 74
49:6 174
50:6 67
53:2–3 78
54:5 57
55:1 123
55:3 174
56:5 183
57:15 ...... 79, 118
66:2 118

Jeremiah
10:10 172
17:7 96
31:3 116
31:34 161

Lamentations
3:24 117

Ezekiel
7:16 74
16:4–6 175

Daniel
9:23 93
9:24 37
10:11 93
10:19 93
12:2 179

Hosea
5:15 120

Micah
7:19 38

Zechariah
- 3:1–4 94
- 3:7 168

13:1 79

Malachi
- 4:2 70

New Testament

Matthew
- 3:6 180
- 3:16 180
- 4:10 173
- 5:7 .... 87, 88
- 5:8 ...... 56, 91, 92
- 7:7 159
- 8:21 175
- 16:18 179
- 18:15–17 182
- 20:28 177
- 21:25 51
- 24:24 179
- 26:30 180
- 28:19 ..... 96, 172, 180
- 28:20 180

Mark
- 16:16 180

Luke
- 1:77 45

- 15:24 175
- 15:32 175
- 16:22 94

John
- 1:12 174
- 1:13 178
- 1:14 ...... 100, 173
- 1:17 ...... 107, 108
- 2:25 149
- 3:6 175
- 3:8 139
- 3:23 180
- 4:24 83
- 5:1–9 165
- 5:25 175
- 5:28 179
- 5:29 179
- 5:39 172
- 6:37 174
- 6:39 ...... 174, 179
- 6:40 179

Reference	Page
10:11	177
10:15	177
10:30	172
11:24	41
11:25	145, 146
15:3	91
15:26	173
17:21	57
20:22	173
20:26	173
21:15–17	149

Acts

Reference	Page
2:1	139
2:23	77
2:41	180
5:3	172
5:4	172
8:8	180
8:12	180
8:31-34	180
8:36	180
8:37	180
8:38	180
8:39	180
9:11	125
16:25	180
17:11	172
17:31	179
24:15	179
24:15–16	40
24:16	181
27:23–24	93

Romans

Reference	Page
1:1	51
1:3	51
1:9	52
3:23	175
3:25	178
3:28	178
4:2	112
4:6	178
4:16	40
4:25	177
5:5	116
5:9	49
5:12	175
5:14	175
5:16-19	178
5:18	175, 176
5:19	175
6:4	180
6:23	176
7:24-25	176
8:1	47, 177
8:2	176
8:3	173, 177
8:4	177
8:7	175
8:8	175
8:26–27	132
8:28	48

8:30....49, 174, 177, 179
8:32.............. 173
8:33........ 47, 177
8:34........ 47, 177
8:39.............. 58
9:5................ 172
9:16.............. 178
10:4............... 50
10:10............ 171
10:14............ 165
12:9.............. 182
12:10............ 182
12:15............ 182
12:16............ 182
15:1.............. 182
15:14............ 182

1 Corinthians
1:30.............. 177
3:16.............. 172
3:17.............. 172
3:22.............. 153
8:6................ 172
11:23–26..... 180
12:26............ 182
13:13.... 141, 143
14:15............ 180
15:3.............. 177
15:13–17....... 39
15:18–19....... 39
15:22............ 175

15:26............154
15:32..............40
15:42–43......154
15:45...........176
15:47...........176
15:55...........154
15:57...........154

2 Corinthians
1:9–10............40
1:20..............109
3:17......132, 172
3:18.............172
6:14–16.........55

Galatians
1:12................52
4:4.................174
4:5.................174
4:6.................173
5:6.................148

Ephesians
1:3.................174
1:3–6............104
1:4.................174
1:5.................174
1:7 104, 177, 178
1:11..............104
1:13–14........105
1:14..............105
1:19..............178
2:3........175, 176
3:1.................175

3:17 59
3:17–18 59
4:1–3 182
4:3–6 97
4:12 182
5:2 177
5:19 180
6:12 94
6:18 182
6:19 182

Philippians
1:27 181
2:2 182
2:3 182
2:4 182
2:6 172
2:13 178
3:10 ...... 111, 112
4:18 70
4:19 134

Colossians
1:10 71
2:2 58
2:12 180
2:13 178
3:1 113
3:3 174
3:4 174
3:13 182
3:16 .... 52, 180
4:5 181

1 Thessalonians
1:4 174
4:13–14 .... 26, 41
4:15-17 179
5:14 182

2 Thessalonians
1:7–10 179
2:8 100
2:13 174
2:13–14 103
3:1 182

1 Timothy
2:5 172
4:8 83

2 Timothy
1:9 .... 174, 178
1:10 176
3:15–17 172
4:1 179

Titus
1:8 52
2:12 181
3:7 49

Hebrews
1:3 173
2:13 179
2:14 176
2:16 176
2:17 176
4:16 133
7:3 78

7:22 176	2 Peter
9:27 ...... 153, 175	1:19 172
9:28 179	1:20 172
10:24 182	1:21 172
10:25 182	1 John
10:29 78	1:3 61
10:37 161	1:7 178
11:1 148	1:9 178
12:14 56	3:1 174
12:24 176	4:13 58
12:25 51	5:7 .... 172, 173
James	5:20 172
1:18 178	Jude
4:8 134	1:1 174
5:13 181	1:3 181
1 Peter	1:24 179
1:2 103	Revelation
1:3 178	1:4–5 96
1:5 179	5:8 70
1:12 51	5:9 177
2:2 117	8:3–4 70
3:4 163	14:13 153
3:18 177	21:6 ...... 121, 122

Classics of Reformed Spirituality

To honour God:
The spirituality of Oliver Cromwell

The revived puritan:
The spirituality of George Whitefield

The armies of the Lamb:
The spirituality of Andrew Fuller

Joy unspeakable and full of glory:
The piety of Samuel and Sarah Pearce

Bespangled with divine grace:
The spirituality of John Gill

www.ingramcontent.com/pod-product-compliance
Lightning Source LLC
Chambersburg PA
CBHW072052110526
44590CB00018B/3132